ἈΡΙΣΤΟΦΑΝΟΥΣ ARISTOPHANES'

Ἱππεῖς *Knights*

A Dual Language Edition

Greek Text Edited by
F. W. Hall and W. M. Geldart

English Translation and Notes by
Ian Johnston

Edited by
Evan Hayes and Stephen Nimis

Faenum Publishing
Oxford, Ohio

Aristophanes' Knights*: A Dual Language Edition*
First Edition

ISBN-10: 194099795X
ISBN-13: 9781940997957

Published by Faenum Publishing, Ltd.
Cover Design: Evan Hayes

for Geoffrey (1974-1997)

οἵη περ φύλλων γενεὴ τοίη δὲ καὶ ἀνδρῶν.
φύλλα τὰ μέν τ' ἄνεμος χαμάδις χέει, ἄλλα δέ θ' ὕλη
τηλεθόωσα φύει, ἔαρος δ' ἐπιγίγνεται ὥρη:
ὣς ἀνδρῶν γενεὴ ἣ μὲν φύει ἣ δ' ἀπολήγει.

Generations of men are like the leaves.
In winter, winds blow them down to earth,
but then, when spring season comes again,
the budding wood grows more. And so with men:
one generation grows, another dies away. (*Iliad* 6)

TABLE OF CONTENTS

EDITORS' NOTE

This book presents the Greek text of Aristophanes' *Knights* with a facing English translation. The Greek text is that of F. W. Hall and W. M. Geldart, (1907), from the Oxford Classical Texts series, which is in the public domain and available as a pdf. This text has also been digitized by the Perseus Project (perseus.tufts.edu). The English translation and accompanying notes are those of Ian Johnston of Vancouver Island University, Nanaimo, BC. This translation is available freely online (records.viu.ca/~-johnstoi/). We have reset both texts, making a number of very minor corrections, and placed them on opposing pages. This facing-page format will be useful to those wishing to read the English translation while looking at the Greek version, or vice versa.

Note that some discrepancies exists between the Greek text and English translation. Occasionally readings from other editions of or commentaries on Aristophanes' Greek text are used, accounting for some minor departures from Hall and Geldart's edition.

INTRODUCTORY NOTE

Aristophanes' *Knights* is a sharp, bawdy, and, in some places, grim satiric allegory on Athenian political life. While the targets of the satire are clear enough, the translator or editor is forced to make some decisions about the names of the characters, because specific names are given only to Demos (whose name means "the people") and to the chorus of Knights.

The main butt of the jokes is clearly Cleon, the popular demagogue of Athenian politics, but the character who represents him is called the Paphlagonian, and Cleon's name is mentioned only once in the play. The term Paphlagonian refers not to an origin in Asia Minor but to his very aggressive rhetoric, since the name comes from the verb meaning "to bluster." The Paphlagonian's main opponent, the Sausage Seller, does have a name (Agoracritus, meaning "chosen by the marketplace"), but that fact does not emerge until very late in the play. Hence, I have used the terms Paphlagonian and Sausage Seller to indicate these characters (some other editions of the play use the names Cleon and Agoracritus throughout).

The two slaves who open the play are not named specifically in the manuscripts, but traditionally they have been called Demosthenes and Nicias, after the two Athenian generals who were enemies of Cleon. I have retained these names because that seemed better than making up alternatives or calling them Slave A and Slave B.

The term "Knights" refers to an elite group of about a thousand cavalry in the Athenian military forces. Each Knight had to provide his own horse and would have expenses he would have to pay himself. However, membership was considered socially prestigious and would be drawn from the richer, more aristocratic Athenians, who tended to be hostile to the populist demagogue Cleon.

At the time *Knights* was first produced (424 BC), Athens and Sparta had been at war for about seven years. The previous year Athens had won an important victory at Pylos against the Spartans, capturing a number of prisoners and bringing them back to Athens. Cleon engineered things so that he received the major credit for this success. As a result, he acquired considerable popularity and was awarded a number of state honours. However, in the view of many Athenians he had, in effect, stolen the credit from Demosthenes. This point is frequently mentioned in the play.

Knights was awarded first prize in the drama competition at the Lenaea festival in 424 BC.

ΙΠΠΕΙΣ

KNIGHTS

ΤΑ ΤΟΥ ΔΡΑΜΑΤΟΣ ΠΡΟΣΩΠΑ

ΔΗΜΟΣΘΕΝΗΣ

ΝΙΚΙΑΣ

ΑΛΛΑΝΤΟΠΩΛΗΣ

ΠΑΦΛΑΓΩΝ

ΔΗΜΟΣ

ΧΟΡΟΣ

DRAMATIS PERSONAE

DEMOSTHENES: a slave in the service of Demos

NICIAS: a slave in the service of Demos

SAUSAGE SELLER: a low-born Athenian street merchant

PAPHLAGONIAN: a slave in the service of Demos

DEMOS: an elderly Athenian citizen

CHORUS OF KNIGHTS.

Ἱππεῖς

ΔΗΜΟΣΘΕΝΗΣ

ἰατταταιὰξ τῶν κακῶν, ἰατταταῖ.
κακῶς Παφλαγόνα τὸν νεώνητον κακὸν
αὐταῖσι βουλαῖς ἀπολέσειαν οἱ θεοί.
ἐξ οὗ γὰρ εἰσήρρησεν ἐς τὴν οἰκίαν
πληγὰς ἀεὶ προστρίβεται τοῖς οἰκέταις.

ΝΙΚΙΑΣ

κάκιστα δῆθ' οὗτός γε πρῶτος Παφλαγόνων
αὐταῖς διαβολαῖς.

ΔΗΜΟΣΘΕΝΗΣ

ὦ κακόδαιμον πῶς ἔχεις;

ΝΙΚΙΑΣ

κακῶς καθάπερ σύ.

ΔΗΜΟΣΘΕΝΗΣ

δεῦρο δὴ πρόσελθ', ἵνα
ξυναυλίαν κλαύσωμεν Οὐλύμπου νόμον.

ΔΗΜΟΣΘΕΝΗΣ *καὶ* ΝΙΚΙΑΣ

μυμῦ μυμῦ μυμῦ μυμῦ μυμῦ μυμῦ.

Knights

[The action takes place in an Athenian street in the Pnyx, the part of the city where the public assemblies were held. At the back there is an entrance to the house belonging to Demos. From within the house comes the noise of a slave being beaten with a whip and crying out in pain.]

Demosthenes *[bursting through the door]*
All right, that's it, that's just too much to take!
I've had it! That bastard interloper!
That miserable Paphlagonian!
I wish the gods would obliterate him—
him and his schemes! Since that awful day
he came into this house, because of him
we slaves keep getting beaten all the time.

Nicias *[coming out behind Demosthenes, in obvious pain]*
That man is the very worst—a first-class
Paphlagonian—all those lies he tells!

Demosthenes
Hey, you poor man, how you doing?

Nicias
Not good.
The same as you.

Demosthenes
All right, come over here,
so we can moan together, pipe a tune,
a duet in the manner of Olympus.

[Demosthenes and Nicias put their heads together and act as if they are both playing flutes, making whimpering sounds in harmony.]

Demosthenes *and* Nicias
What can we do-o-ooooo,
We're just so black and blue-oo-oo.[1]

Δημοσθενης

τί κινυρόμεθ' ἄλλως; οὐκ ἐχρῆν ζητεῖν τινα
σωτηρίαν νῷν, ἀλλὰ μὴ κλάειν ἔτι;

Νικιας

τίς οὖν γένοιτ' ἄν;

Δημοσθενης

λέγε σύ.

Νικιας

σὺ μὲν οὖν μοι λέγε,
ἵνα μὴ μάχωμαι.

Δημοσθενης

μὰ τὸν Ἀπόλλω 'γὼ μὲν οὔ.

Νικιας

πῶς ἂν σύ μοι λέξειας ἁμὲ χρὴ λέγειν;

Δημοσθενης

ἀλλ' εἰπὲ θαρρῶν, εἶτα κἀγὼ σοὶ φράσω.

Νικιας

ἀλλ' οὐκ ἔνι μοι τὸ θρέττε. πῶς ἂν οὖν ποτε
εἴποιμ' ἂν αὐτὸ δῆτα κομψευριπικῶς;

Δημοσθενης

μὴ 'μοί γε, μὴ 'μοί, μὴ διασκανδικίσῃς·
ἀλλ' εὑρέ τιν' ἀπόκινον ἀπὸ τοῦ δεσπότου.

Νικιας

λέγε δὴ μόλωμεν ξυνεχὲς ὡδὶ ξυλλαβών.

DEMOSTHENES

Why waste our time moaning? We should stop
and look for some way to preserve our hides.

NICIAS

How could we do that?

DEMOSTHENES

Well, suggest something.

NICIAS

No, you tell me—that way I can avoid
fighting you about it.

[Here Demosthenes and Nicias briefly parody the grand tragic style.]

DEMOSTHENES

No. By Apollo. No.

I shall not speak.

NICIAS

Ah, if only you would tell me

what I should say.

DEMOSTHENES

Come. Screw your courage up

and speak. And then I shall confide in you.

NICIAS

But I dare not. How could I ever utter
the delicate phrasings of Euripides—
"Can't thou not speak for me what I must say"?[2]

DEMOSTHENES

No, I don't want that. Don't toss those herbs around.
Instead find us some way we can dance off
and leave our master.[3]

NICIAS *[miming masturbation]*

Then say, "Let's beat off"—

all in one word, as I do.

ΔΗΜΟΣΘΕΝΗΣ

καὶ δὴ λέγω μόλωμεν.

ΝΙΚΙΑΣ

ἐξόπισθε νῦν
αὐτὸ φάθι τοῦ μόλωμεν.

ΔΗΜΟΣΘΕΝΗΣ

αὐτό.

ΝΙΚΙΑΣ

πάνυ καλῶς.
ὥσπερ δεφόμενος νῦν ἀτρέμα πρῶτον λέγε
τὸ μόλωμεν, εἶτα δ' αὐτό, κᾆτ' ἐπάγων πυκνόν.

ΔΗΜΟΣΘΕΝΗΣ

μόλωμεν αὐτὸ μόλωμεν αὐτομολῶμεν.

ΝΙΚΙΑΣ

ἦν
οὐχ ἡδύ;

ΔΗΜΟΣΘΕΝΗΣ

νὴ Δία· πλήν γε περὶ τῷ δέρματι
δέδοικα τουτονὶ τὸν οἰωνόν.

ΝΙΚΙΑΣ

τί δαί;

ΔΗΜΟΣΘΕΝΗΣ

ὁτιὴ τὸ δέρμα δεφομένων ἀπέρχεται.

ΝΙΚΙΑΣ

κράτιστα τοίνυν τῶν παρόντων ἐστὶ νῷν,
θεῶν ἰόντε προσπεσεῖν του πρὸς βρέτας.

DEMOSTHENES *[copying Nicias]*
All right, then,
I say, "Let's beat off."

NICIAS
Now after "Let's beat off,"
say "out of here."

DEMOSTHENES
"Out of here."

NICIAS
Very good.
It's like when you give yourself a hand job—
at first you say it gently, "Let's beat off,"
then you quickly speed it up—"out of here."

DEMOSTHENES *[copying the gesture]*
Let's beat off . . . out of here, let's beat off . . .

[Finally he sees what Nicias is getting at.]
Ah, we beat off out of here—we run away!

NICIAS
Well, what about it? Doesn't that sound sweet?

DEMOSTHENES
Yes, by god, it does—except for one thing:
I'm terrified that beating it like this
might be a prophecy about my skin.[4]

NICIAS
Why's that?

DEMOSTHENES
Because when you pound your snake
the skin comes off.

NICIAS
The way things are right now
the best thing we can do is head on out
and throw ourselves down before some statue
of a god.

ΔΗΜΟΣΘΕΝΗΣ

† ποῖον βρέτας †; ἐτεὸν ἡγεῖ γὰρ θεούς;

ΝΙΚΙΑΣ

ἔγωγε.

ΔΗΜΟΣΘΕΝΗΣ

ποίῳ χρώμενος τεκμηρίῳ;

ΝΙΚΙΑΣ

ὁτιὴ θεοῖσιν ἐχθρός εἰμ᾽. οὐκ εἰκότως;

ΔΗΜΟΣΘΕΝΗΣ

εὖ προσβιβάζεις μ᾽. ἀλλ᾽ ἑτέρᾳ πῃ σκεπτέον.
βούλει τὸ πρᾶγμα τοῖς θεαταῖσιν φράσω;

ΝΙΚΙΑΣ

οὐ χεῖρον· ἓν δ᾽ αὐτοὺς παραιτησώμεθα,
ἐπίδηλον ἡμῖν τοῖς προσώποισιν ποιεῖν,
ἢν τοῖς ἔπεσι χαίρωσι καὶ τοῖς πράγμασιν.

ΔΗΜΟΣΘΕΝΗΣ

λέγοιμ᾽ ἂν ἤδη. νῷν γάρ ἐστι δεσπότης
ἄγροικος ὀργὴν κυαμοτρὼξ ἀκράχολος,
Δῆμος πυκνίτης, δύσκολον γερόντιον
ὑπόκωφον. οὗτος τῇ προτέρᾳ νουμηνίᾳ
ἐπρίατο δοῦλον, βυρσοδέψην Παφλαγόνα,
πανουργότατον καὶ διαβολώτατόν τινα.
οὗτος καταγνοὺς τοῦ γέροντος τοὺς τρόπους,
ὁ βυρσοπαφλαγών, ὑποπεσὼν τὸν δεσπότην
ᾔκαλλ᾽ ἐθώπευ᾽ ἐκολάκευ᾽ ἐξηπάτα
κοσκυλματίοις ἄκροισι τοιαυτὶ λέγων·

DEMOSTHENES

A statue? What kind of statue?
Do you really believe that there are gods?

NICIAS

Of course I do.

DEMOSTHENES

What sort of evidence
have you got for that?

NICIAS

Well, I'm someone
gods clearly do not like. Does that not count
as confirmation?[5]

DEMOSTHENES

Proof enough for me.
So we'd better look someplace else for help.
Do you want me to tell this audience
what's going on?

NICIAS

That's not a bad idea.
We could ask them to do one thing for us—
show us by their faces if they enjoy
what we say and do.

DEMOSTHENES

Then I'll speak up.

[He directs his explanation to the audience.]

We have a bad tempered and crude master.
He chews beans and is angry all the time—
Demos of the Pnyx, a grumpy old man
who's half deaf.[6] Last new moon he bought a slave,
a Paphlagonian tanner, a great scoundrel,
the most slanderous of rogues.[7] And this slave,
this tanner from Paphlagonia, observed
the old man's habits. He threw himself down
at our master's feet and began fawning,
wheedling, flattering, buttering him up
with tiny scraps of leather, saying things like

ὦ Δῆμε λοῦσαι πρῶτον ἐκδικάσας μίαν,
ἐνθοῦ ῥόφησον ἔντραγ' ἔχε τριώβολον.
βούλει παραθῶ σοι δόρπον; εἶτ' ἀναρπάσας
ὅ τι ἄν τις ἡμῶν σκευάσῃ, τῷ δεσπότῃ
Παφλαγὼν κεχάρισται τοῦτο. καὶ πρώην γ' ἐμοῦ
μᾶζαν μεμαχότος ἐν Πύλῳ Λακωνικήν,
πανουργότατά πως περιδραμὼν ὑφαρπάσας
αὐτὸς παρέθηκε τὴν ὑπ' ἐμοῦ μεμαγμένην,
ἡμᾶς δ' ἀπελαύνει κοὐκ ἐᾷ τὸν δεσπότην
ἄλλον θεραπεύειν, ἀλλὰ βυρσίνην ἔχων
δειπνοῦντος ἑστὼς ἀποσοβεῖ τοὺς ῥήτορας.
ᾄδει δὲ χρησμούς· ὁ δὲ γέρων σιβυλλιᾷ.
ὁ δ' αὐτὸν ὡς ὁρᾷ μεμακκοακότα,
τέχνην πεποίηται. τοὺς γὰρ ἔνδον ἄντικρυς
ψευδῆ διαβάλλει· κᾆτα μαστιγούμεθα
ἡμεῖς· Παφλαγὼν δὲ περιθέων τοὺς οἰκέτας
αἰτεῖ ταράττει δωροδοκεῖ λέγων τάδε·
'ὁρᾶτε τὸν Ὕλαν δι' ἐμὲ μαστιγούμενον;
εἰ μή μ' ἀναπείσετ', ἀποθανεῖσθε τήμερον.'
ἡμεῖς δὲ δίδομεν· εἰ δὲ μή, πατούμενοι
ὑπὸ τοῦ γέροντος ὀκταπλάσιον χέζομεν.
νῦν οὖν ἀνύσαντε φροντίσωμεν ὦγαθέ,
ποίαν ὁδὸν νὼ τρεπτέον καὶ πρὸς τίνα.

ΝΙΚΙΑΣ

κράτιστ' ἐκείνην τὴν μόλωμεν ὦγαθέ.

ΔΗΜΟΣΘΕΝΗΣ

ἀλλ' οὐχ οἷόν τε τὸν Παφλαγόν' οὐδὲν λαθεῖν·
ἐφορᾷ γὰρ οὗτος πάντ'. ἔχει γὰρ τὸ σκέλος

"O Demos, once you've tried a single case
then take a bath," "Taste this," "Gulp this down,"
"Eat up," "Take three obols," "Would you like me
to get an evening meal brought in for you?"[8]
Then that Paphlagonian grabs from one of us
something we've prepared and offers it up
to our master. Just a few days ago,
when I'd kneaded a Spartan barley cake
at Pylos, that devilish rogue somehow
snuck past me, grabbed the cake I had just made,
and presented it as his.[9] He makes sure
we keep our distance and will not allow
anyone else to attend on Demos.
When our master's eating dinner, he stands
holding a leather thong and flicks away
the orators. He chants out oracles,
so the old man is mad for prophecies,
and when he sees that he's quite lost his wits,
he goes to work according to his plan—
accusing those inside with outright lies,
so we get whipped, while that Paphlagonian
scampers among the slaves, making demands,
stirring up trouble, taking bribes. He'll say,
"You see how I set things up so Hylas
got a beating. If you don't win me over,
then you're dead meat today."[10] So we pay up.
If we don't, the old man abuses us,
and we shit out eight times as much.

[Demosthenes turns back to Nicias.]

So now,
my friend, let's come up with something fast—
what path or person can we turn to now?

NICIAS

The best way, my friend, is that beating off—
getting out of here.

DEMOSTHENES

But there's no damn way
we can escape the Paphlagonian.
That man sees everything. He has one leg

τὸ μὲν ἐν Πύλῳ, τὸ δ᾽ ἕτερον ἐν τἠκκλησίᾳ.
τοσόνδε δ᾽ αὐτοῦ βῆμα διαβεβηκότος
ὁ πρωκτός ἐστιν αὐτόχρημ᾽ ἐν Χάοσιν,
τὼ χεῖρ᾽ ἐν Αἰτωλοῖς, ὁ νοῦς δ᾽ ἐν Κλωπιδῶν.

ΝΙΚΙΑΣ

κράτιστον οὖν νῷν ἀποθανεῖν.

ΔΗΜΟΣΘΕΝΗΣ

ἀλλὰ σκόπει,
ὅπως ἂν ἀποθάνοιμεν ἀνδρικώτατα.

ΝΙΚΙΑΣ

πῶς δῆτα πῶς γένοιτ᾽ ἂν ἀνδρικώτατα;
βέλτιστον ἡμῖν αἷμα ταύρειον πιεῖν.
ὁ Θεμιστοκλέους γὰρ θάνατος αἱρετώτερος.

ΔΗΜΟΣΘΕΝΗΣ

μὰ Δί᾽ ἀλλ᾽ ἄκρατον οἶνον ἀγαθοῦ δαίμονος.
ἴσως γὰρ ἂν χρηστόν τι βουλευσαίμεθα.

ΝΙΚΙΑΣ

ἰδού γ᾽ ἄκρατον. περὶ πότου γοῦν ἐστί σοι;
πῶς δ᾽ ἂν μεθύων χρηστόν τι βουλεύσαιτ᾽ ἀνήρ;

ΔΗΜΟΣΘΕΝΗΣ

ἄληθες οὗτος; κρουνοχυτρολήραιον εἶ.
οἶνον σὺ τολμᾷς εἰς ἐπίνοιαν λοιδορεῖν;
οἴνου γὰρ εὕροις ἄν τι πρακτικώτερον;
ὁρᾷς, ὅταν πίνωσιν ἄνθρωποι τότε

in Pylos, and he keeps his other leg
in the assembly—his two feet are spread
this far apart.

[Demosthenes demonstrates his words by almost doing the splits and keeps talking from an awkward position, which gets worse as he goes on.]

His arsehole is right here
over the Chaones, his hands are there,
in Aetolia, and his mind is over here,
among the Clopidians.[11]

NICIAS

Then the best thing
for us would be to die.

DEMOSTHENES *[straightening up]*

All right, let's see.
The most manly way we two could perish—
what would that be?

NICIAS

The most courageous way?
The best would be for us to drink bull's blood—
that's a good one to choose. Themistocles
died from that.[12]

DEMOSTHENES

No, by god, not that. But wine—
undiluted from the Good Spirit cup!
Then perhaps we'll think of something useful.[13]

NICIAS

O yes, unmixed wine! It's natural you'd think
of having a drink. But can anyone
come up with good advice when he is drunk?

DEMOSTHENES

What a thing to ask! Bah! You're a fountain
spouting streams of streaming bullshit! You dare
complain that wine disturbs the way we think?
What can you find better than some wine
for getting men to act effectively?
You see that when men drink, they get wealthy,

πλουτοῦσι διαπράττουσι νικῶσιν δίκας
εὐδαιμονοῦσιν ὠφελοῦσι τοὺς φίλους.
ἀλλ' ἐξένεγκέ μοι ταχέως οἴνου χοᾶ,
τὸν νοῦν ἵν' ἄρδω καὶ λέγω τι δεξιόν.

ΝΙΚΙΑΣ

οἴμοι τί ποθ' ἡμᾶς ἐργάσει τῷ σῷ πότῳ;

ΔΗΜΟΣΘΕΝΗΣ

ἀγάθ'· ἀλλ' ἔνεγκ'· ἐγὼ δὲ κατακλινήσομαι.
ἢν γὰρ μεθυσθῶ, πάντα ταυτὶ καταπάσω
βουλευματίων καὶ γνωμιδίων καὶ νοιδίων.

ΝΙΚΙΑΣ

ὡς εὐτυχῶς ὅτι οὐκ ἐλήφθην ἔνδοθεν
κλέπτων τὸν οἶνον.

ΔΗΜΟΣΘΕΝΗΣ

εἰπέ μοι Παφλαγὼν τί δρᾷ;

ΝΙΚΙΑΣ

ἐπίπαστα λείξας δημιόπραθ' ὁ βάσκανος
ῥέγκει μεθύων ἐν ταῖσι βύρσαις ὕπτιος.

ΔΗΜΟΣΘΕΝΗΣ

ἴθι νυν ἄκρατον ἐγκάναξόν μοι πολὺν
σπονδήν.

ΝΙΚΙΑΣ

λαβὲ δὴ καὶ σπεῖσον ἀγαθοῦ δαίμονος.

ΔΗΜΟΣΘΕΝΗΣ

ἕλχ' ἕλκε τὴν τοῦ δαίμονος τοῦ Πραμνίου.
ὦ δαῖμον ἀγαθὲ σὸν τὸ βούλευμ', οὐκ ἐμόν.

they are successful, they win their lawsuits,
they become happy and help out their friends.
Come, bring me out a jug of wine right now,
so I can refresh my mind and think up
something really clever.

NICIAS

By all the gods,
what will you end up doing to both of us
with this drinking of yours?

DEMOSTHENES

Something good.
Go get it, while I sit myself down right here.

[Nicias goes into the house.]

For if I do get drunk, then I'll spatter
tiny schemes and fancies, miniscule ideas,
in all directions.

[Nicias returns from the house with large jug of wine and a cup.]

NICIAS

It's a good thing
I wasn't caught in there stealing this wine.

DEMOSTHENES

Tell me—what's the Paphlagonian doing?

NICIAS

That slanderous rogue has been licking up
some cake he confiscated. Now he's drunk—
lying on his back, snoring on his hides.

DEMOSTHENES

Well, come on then, pour me a generous hit
of that unmixed wine . . . for a libation.[14]

NICIAS *[pouring out the wine]*

There. Take it and offer a libation
to the Good Spirit.

DEMOSTHENES *[smelling and then gulping down the wine]*

Drink this and swill down
the fine Pramnian spirit.[15] O excellent Spirit,
the idea is yours—not mine.

Νικιας

εἴπ', ἀντιβολῶ, τί ἔστι;

Δημοσθενης

τοὺς χρησμοὺς ταχὺ
κλέψας ἔνεγκε τοῦ Παφλαγόνος ἔνδοθεν,
ἕως καθεύδει.

Νικιας

ταῦτ'. ἀτὰρ τοῦ δαίμονος
δέδοιχ' ὅπως μὴ τεύξομαι κακοδαίμονος.

Δημοσθενης

φέρε νυν ἐγὼ μ' αὐτῷ προσαγάγω τὸν χοᾶ.
τὸν νοῦν ἵν' ἄρδω καὶ λέγω τι δεξιόν.

Νικιας

ὡς μεγάλ' ὁ Παφλαγὼν πέρδεται καὶ ῥέγκεται,
ὥστ' ἔλαθον αὐτὸν τὸν ἱερὸν χρησμὸν λαβών,
ὅνπερ μάλιστ' ἐφύλαττεν.

Δημοσθενης

ὦ σοφώτατε.
φέρ' αὐτὸν ἵν' ἀναγνῶ· σὺ δ' ἔγχεον πιεῖν
ἀνύσας τι. φέρ' ἴδω τί ἄρ' ἔνεστιν αὐτόθι.
ὦ λόγια. δός μοι δὸς τὸ ποτήριον ταχύ.

Νικιας

ἰδού. τί φησ' ὁ χρησμός;

Δημοσθενης

ἑτέραν ἔγχεον.

NICIAS

All right tell me.
I'm asking you. What is that great idea?

DEMOSTHENES

Get inside there and steal the oracles
belonging to the Paphlagonian—
quickly while he's asleep.[16]

NICIAS

All right, I'll go.
But I'm afraid I might find this Good Spirit
becomes the genius of my misfortune.

[Nicias goes back into the house]

DEMOSTHENES

Let's see now—I'll bring this jug over here
beside me so I can moisten my mind
and come up with some fabulous idea.

[Demosthenes takes another drink. Nicias comes back from the house with a scroll.]

NICIAS

That Paphlagonian—what a noise he makes
farting and snoring. Thanks to that I grabbed
the sacred oracle, the one he guards
so carefully, without him noticing.

DEMOSTHENES

You are the craftiest of men! Give it here,
so I can look it over—and pour me
a drink. Hurry up! Well now, let me see.
What's in here?

[Demosthenes reads the scroll.]

O these prophecies! Quick!
Give me a drink! Come on!

NICIAS *[pouring the wine]*

Here you go. Well?
What does the oracle say?

DEMOSTHENES *[draining the cup and holding it out]*

Pour me another.

ΝΙΚΙΑΣ

ἐν τοῖς λογίοις ἔνεστιν 'ἑτέραν ἔγχεον;'

ΔΗΜΟΣΘΕΝΗΣ

ὦ Βάκι.

ΝΙΚΙΑΣ

τί ἔστι;

ΔΗΜΟΣΘΕΝΗΣ

δὸς τὸ ποτήριον ταχύ.

ΝΙΚΙΑΣ

πολλῷ γ' ὁ Βάκις ἐχρῆτο τῷ ποτηρίῳ.

ΔΗΜΟΣΘΕΝΗΣ

ὦ μιαρὲ Παφλαγὼν ταῦτ' ἄρ' ἐφυλάττου πάλαι,
τὸν περὶ σεαυτοῦ χρησμὸν ὀρρωδῶν;

ΝΙΚΙΑΣ

τιή;

ΔΗΜΟΣΘΕΝΗΣ

ἐνταῦθ' ἔνεστιν, αὐτὸς ὡς ἀπόλλυται.

ΝΙΚΙΑΣ

καὶ πῶς;

ΔΗΜΟΣΘΕΝΗΣ

ὅπως; ὁ χρησμὸς ἄντικρυς λέγει
ὡς πρῶτα μὲν στυππειοπώλης γίγνεται,
ὃς πρῶτος ἕξει τῆς πόλεως τὰ πράγματα.

ΝΙΚΙΑΣ

εἷς οὑτοσὶ πώλης. τί τοὐντεῦθεν; λέγε.

ΔΗΜΟΣΘΕΝΗΣ

μετὰ τοῦτον αὖθις προβατοπώλης δεύτερος.

Nicias *[taking the cup]*
That's what it says there? "Pour another drink"?

Demosthenes
O Bacis![17]

Nicias *[pouring out more wine]*
What is it?

Demosthenes
Quick! Pass me that cup!

Nicias
Bacis really gets to use that cup a lot.

Demosthenes *[looking at the scroll]*
O you disgraceful Paphlagonian!
So that's why you've been protecting yourself
all this time! You're terrified of this oracle—
it's about you!

Nicias
Why's that?

Demosthenes
In here it says
how he's to be destroyed.

Nicias
And how is that?

Demosthenes
How? Well, this oracle clearly predicts
that first a dealer in hemp will come along
and, to start with, control city business.[18]

Nicias
That's one wheeler dealer. So who comes next?
Tell me.

Demosthenes
After that one comes another—
someone who deals in sheep.[19]

ΝΙΚΙΑΣ

δύο τώδε πώλα. καὶ τί τόνδε χρὴ παθεῖν;

ΔΗΜΟΣΘΕΝΗΣ

κρατεῖν, ἕως ἕτερος ἀνὴρ βδελυρώτερος
αὐτοῦ γένοιτο· μετὰ δὲ ταῦτ' ἀπόλλυται.
ἐπιγίγνεται γὰρ βυρσοπώλης ὁ Παφλαγών,
ἅρπαξ κεκράκτης Κυκλοβόρου φωνὴν ἔχων.

ΝΙΚΙΑΣ

τὸν προβατοπώλην ἦν ἄρ' ἀπολέσθαι χρεὼν
ὑπὸ βυρσοπώλου;

ΔΗΜΟΣΘΕΝΗΣ

νὴ Δί'.

ΝΙΚΙΑΣ

οἴμοι δείλαιος.
πόθεν οὖν ἂν ἔτι γένοιτο πώλης εἷς μόνος;

ΔΗΜΟΣΘΕΝΗΣ

ἔτ' ἐστὶν εἷς ὑπερφυᾶ τέχνην ἔχων.

ΝΙΚΙΑΣ

εἴπ', ἀντιβολῶ, τίς ἐστιν;

ΔΗΜΟΣΘΕΝΗΣ

εἴπω;

ΝΙΚΙΑΣ

νὴ Δία.

ΔΗΜΟΣΘΕΝΗΣ

ἀλλαντοπώλης ἔσθ' ὁ τοῦτον ἐξολῶν.

ΝΙΚΙΑΣ

ἀλλαντοπώλης; ὦ Πόσειδον τῆς τέχνης.
φέρε ποῦ τὸν ἄνδρα τοῦτον ἐξευρήσομεν;

Nicias

That's two dealers.
What's supposed to happen to that second one?

Demosthenes

He's to be in charge until someone else,
a more repulsive man, comes on the scene.
Once that happens, he dies. His successor
is a leather dealer and a robber,
a Paphlagonian with a screaming voice,
like the raging stream of Cycloborus.[20]

Nicias

So Fate decreed that the dealer in sheep
would be toppled by the leather dealer?

Demosthenes

That's right.

Nicias

Then heaven help us—we're in trouble!
I wish some other dealer might show up
from somewhere—just one!

Demosthenes

Well, there is one—
he has a splendid trade.

Nicias

Tell me who that is.
Come on, I'm asking you.

Demosthenes

Want me to tell you?

Nicias

Yes. For god's sake!

Demosthenes *[reading from the scroll]*

The man who will destroy
the Paphlagonian is a sausage dealer.

Nicias

A sausage dealer? O Poseidon, what a trade!
Where on earth do we find a man like that?

ΔΗΜΟΣΘΕΝΗΣ

ζητῶμεν αὐτόν.

ΝΙΚΙΑΣ

ἀλλ᾽ ὁδὶ προσέρχεται
ὥσπερ κατὰ θεὸν εἰς ἀγοράν.

ΔΗΜΟΣΘΕΝΗΣ

ὦ μακάριε
ἀλλαντοπῶλα, δεῦρο δεῦρ᾽ ὦ φίλτατε
ἀνάβαινε σωτὴρ τῇ πόλει καὶ νῷν φανείς.

ΑΛΛΑΝΤΟΠΩΛΗΣ

τί ἔστι; τί με καλεῖτε;

ΔΗΜΟΣΘΕΝΗΣ

δεῦρ᾽ ἔλθ᾽, ἵνα πύθῃ
ὡς εὐτυχὴς εἶ καὶ μεγάλως εὐδαιμονεῖς.

ΝΙΚΙΑΣ

ἴθι δὴ κάθελ᾽ αὐτοῦ τοὐλεὸν καὶ τοῦ θεοῦ
τὸν χρησμὸν ἀναδίδαξον αὐτὸν ὡς ἔχει·
ἐγὼ δ᾽ ἰὼν προσκέψομαι τὸν Παφλαγόνα.

ΔΗΜΟΣΘΕΝΗΣ

ἄγε δὴ σὺ κατάθου πρῶτα τὰ σκεύη χαμαί·
ἔπειτα τὴν γῆν πρόσκυσον καὶ τοὺς θεούς.

ΑΛΛΑΝΤΟΠΩΛΗΣ

ἰδού· τί ἔστιν;

ΔΗΜΟΣΘΕΝΗΣ

ὦ μακάρι᾽ ὦ πλούσιε,

DEMOSTHENES
Let's go look for him.

[Enter the Sausage Seller carrying a table, knives, sausages, and so on.]

NICIAS
Hey, there's one coming here,
as if he's off to market. A stroke of luck!

DEMOSTHENES *[calling to the Sausage Seller]*
Hey, sausage seller—you blessed creature.
Come on over here, dear friend—over here.[21]
You show up as a saviour for the city
and for the two of us.

SAUSAGE SELLER
What's going on?
Why are you calling me?

DEMOSTHENES
Come over here,
so you can find out your enormous luck,
how tremendously fortunate you are.

[The Sausage Seller climbs up from the orchestra onto the stage with Demosthenes and Nicias.]

NICIAS
Come on, take that table from him. Tell him
what the god's oracle proclaims. I'll go
and keep watch on the Paphlagonian.

[Nicias exits into the house.]

DEMOSTHENES
All right. First of all, set that equipment down
on the ground here. And make a sacred salute
to the earth and to the gods.[22]

SAUSAGE SELLER *[carrying out those actions]*
There! What's going on?

DEMOSTHENES
O you most blest of men! And wealthy, too!

ὦ νῦν μὲν οὐδεὶς αὔριον δ' ὑπέρμεγας,
ὦ τῶν Ἀθηνῶν ταγὲ τῶν εὐδαιμόνων.

ΑΛΛΑΝΤΟΠΩΛΗΣ

τί μ' ὦγάθ' οὐ πλύνειν ἐᾷς τὰς κοιλίας
πωλεῖν τε τοὺς ἀλλᾶντας, ἀλλὰ καταγελᾷς;

ΔΗΜΟΣΘΕΝΗΣ

ὦ μῶρε ποίας κοιλίας; δευρὶ βλέπε.
τὰς στίχας ὁρᾷς τὰς τῶνδε τῶν λαῶν;

ΑΛΛΑΝΤΟΠΩΛΗΣ

ὁρῶ.

ΔΗΜΟΣΘΕΝΗΣ

τούτων ἁπάντων αὐτὸς ἀρχέλας ἔσει,
καὶ τῆς ἀγορᾶς καὶ τῶν λιμένων καὶ τῆς πυκνός·
βουλὴν πατήσεις καὶ στρατηγοὺς κλαστάσεις,
δήσεις φυλάξεις, ἐν πρυτανείῳ λαικάσει.

ΑΛΛΑΝΤΟΠΩΛΗΣ

ἐγώ;

ΔΗΜΟΣΘΕΝΗΣ

σὺ μέντοι· κοὐδέπω γε πάνθ' ὁρᾷς.
ἀλλ' ἐπανάβηθι κἀπὶ τοὐλεὸν τοδὶ
καὶ κάτιδε τὰς νήσους ἁπάσας ἐν κύκλῳ.

ΑΛΛΑΝΤΟΠΩΛΗΣ

καθορῶ.

ΔΗΜΟΣΘΕΝΗΣ

τί δαί; τἀμπόρια καὶ τὰς ὁλκάδας;

ΑΛΛΑΝΤΟΠΩΛΗΣ

ἔγωγε.

Today you have nothing, but tomorrow
you will be immensely great, chief leader
of a happy Athens!

SAUSAGE SELLER

My good fellow,
why not leave me alone to wash my tripe
and sell my sausages, instead of mocking me?

DEMOSTHENES

You silly fool! Forget about your tripe!
Look over there. Do you see those people,
all those rows?

SAUSAGE SELLER

I see them.

DEMOSTHENES

You're going to be
lord and master of them all, in control
of the marketplaces and the harbours
and of the Pnyx. You'll stomp on the Council,
keep generals in line, tie people up,
throw them in jail—and in the Prytaneum
you'll be sucking cocks.[23]

SAUSAGE SELLER

Me?

DEMOSTHENES

Yes, you of course.
But you're not seeing the whole picture yet.
Climb up on this table of yours—gaze out
at all the islands there surrounding us.

SAUSAGE SELLER *[climbs up on his table and looks out]*
I see them.

DEMOSTHENES

What do you see? Trading ports?
Merchant ships?

SAUSAGE SELLER

Yes. I see those.

ΔΗΜΟΣΘΕΝΗΣ

πῶς οὖν οὐ μεγάλως εὐδαιμονεῖς;
ἔτι νῦν τὸν ὀφθαλμὸν παράβαλλ᾽ ἐς Καρίαν
τὸν δεξιόν, τὸν δ᾽ ἕτερον ἐς Καρχηδόνα.

ΑΛΛΑΝΤΟΠΩΛΗΣ

εὐδαιμονήσω δ᾽ εἰ διαστραφήσομαι;

ΔΗΜΟΣΘΕΝΗΣ

οὐκ ἀλλὰ διὰ σοῦ ταῦτα πάντα πέρναται.
γίγνει γάρ, ὡς ὁ χρησμὸς οὑτοσὶ λέγει,
ἀνὴρ μέγιστος.

ΑΛΛΑΝΤΟΠΩΛΗΣ

εἰπέ μοι καὶ πῶς ἐγὼ
ἀλλαντοπώλης ὢν ἀνὴρ γενήσομαι;

ΔΗΜΟΣΘΕΝΗΣ

δι᾽ αὐτὸ γάρ τοι τοῦτο καὶ γίγνει μέγας,
ὁτιὴ πονηρὸς κἀξ ἀγορᾶς εἶ καὶ θρασύς.

ΑΛΛΑΝΤΟΠΩΛΗΣ

οὐκ ἀξιῶ ᾽γὼ ᾽μαυτὸν ἰσχύειν μέγα.

ΔΗΜΟΣΘΕΝΗΣ

οἴμοι τί ποτ᾽ ἔσθ᾽ ὅτι σαυτὸν οὐ φῄς ἄξιον;
ξυνειδέναι τί μοι δοκεῖς σαυτῷ καλόν.
μῶν ἐκ καλῶν εἶ κἀγαθῶν;

ΑΛΛΑΝΤΟΠΩΛΗΣ

μὰ τοὺς θεοὺς
εἰ μὴ ᾽κ πονηρῶν γ᾽.

ΔΗΜΟΣΘΕΝΗΣ

ὦ μακάριε τῆς τύχης
ὅσον πέπονθας ἀγαθὸν ἐς τὰ πράγματα.

DEMOSTHENES

All right then,
how can you not be immensely fortunate?
Now turn your right eye towards Caria
and the other eye towards Carthage.[24]

SAUSAGE SELLER *[in great physical discomfort]*

I'll be happy
once I dislocate my neck!

DEMOSTHENES

That not the point.
All that land is to be traded away,
thanks to you. For you are going to be
the most powerful of men—this oracle
says so right here.

SAUSAGE SELLER

Then explain this to me—
How am I, a seller of sausages,
going to change to someone respectable?

DEMOSTHENES

The very reason you'll be powerful
is that you're a shameless market rascal—
and impudent, as well.

SAUSAGE SELLER

But I don't think
I'm good enough to have great influence.

DEMOSTHENES

Good heavens, whatever is wrong with you
to make you say you are not good enough?
You must, I'm sure, know something remarkable
about yourself. What about your parents?
Don't you come from good and honest people?

SAUSAGE SELLER

By god no! Nothing but worthless rabble.

DEMOSTHENES

O you fine fellow! Such amazing luck!
For political affairs you really have
such great advantages!

ΑΛΛΑΝΤΟΠΩΛΗΣ

ἀλλ' ὦγάθ' οὐδὲ μουσικὴν ἐπίσταμαι
πλὴν γραμμάτων, καὶ ταῦτα μέντοι κακὰ κακῶς.

ΔΗΜΟΣΘΕΝΗΣ

τουτὶ μόνον σ' ἔβλαψεν, ὅτι καὶ κακὰ κακῶς.
ἡ δημαγωγία γὰρ οὐ πρὸς μουσικοῦ
ἔτ' ἐστὶν ἀνδρὸς οὐδὲ χρηστοῦ τοὺς τρόπους,
ἀλλ' εἰς ἀμαθῆ καὶ βδελυρόν. ἀλλὰ μὴ παρῇς
ἅ σοι διδόασ' ἐν τοῖς λογίοισιν οἱ θεοί.

ΑΛΛΑΝΤΟΠΩΛΗΣ

πῶς δῆτά φησ' ὁ χρησμός;

ΔΗΜΟΣΘΕΝΗΣ

εὖ νὴ τοὺς θεοὺς
καὶ ποικίλως πως καὶ σοφῶς ᾐνιγμένος·
ἀλλ' ὁπόταν μάρψῃ βυρσαίετος ἀγκυλοχήλης
γαμφηλῇσι δράκοντα κοάλεμον αἱματοπώτην,
δὴ τότε Παφλαγόνων μὲν ἀπόλλυται ἡ σκοροδάλμη,
κοιλιοπώλῃσιν δὲ θεὸς μέγα κῦδος ὀπάζει,
αἴ κεν μὴ πωλεῖν ἀλλᾶντας μᾶλλον ἕλωνται.

ΑΛΛΑΝΤΟΠΩΛΗΣ

πῶς οὖν πρὸς ἐμὲ ταῦτ' ἐστίν; ἀναδίδασκέ με.

ΔΗΜΟΣΘΕΝΗΣ

βυρσαίετος μὲν ὁ Παφλαγών ἐσθ' οὑτοσί.

ΑΛΛΑΝΤΟΠΩΛΗΣ

τί δ' ἀγκυλοχήλης ἐστίν;

SAUSAGE SELLER

But, my good man,
I have no education, nothing but
reading and writing, and I'm bad at those—
real bad.

DEMOSTHENES

That's the only thing stopping you,
that you can read and write, even poorly—
real bad. You see, a leader of the people
no longer needs to have any training
or be honest in his dealings. Instead
he should be ignorant and disgusting.
But you must not disregard what the gods
are offering to you in this oracle.

SAUSAGE SELLER

What does the oracle say?

DEMOSTHENES

By the gods,
it's good—but its style is rather intricate,
written as a sophisticated riddle.

[He reads the oracle in a solemn tone.]

"But when the eagle tanner with his crooked claws
shall in his beak seize the stupid, blood-sucking serpent,
then will perish the Paphlagonian's pickled garlic,
and then the gods will bestow enormous fame
on those whose vocation is to market tripe
unless they would prefer to sell their sausages."

SAUSAGE SELLER

How has this got anything to do with me?

DEMOSTHENES

Well, the eagle tanner is that man there—

[Demosthenes points to Cleon sitting in the audience.]

the Paphlagonian . . .

SAUSAGE SELLER

Those "crooked claws"—
what are they?

ΔΗΜΟΣΘΕΝΗΣ

αὐτό που λέγει,
ὅτι ἀγκύλαις ταῖς χερσὶν ἁρπάζων φέρει.

ΑΛΛΑΝΤΟΠΩΛΗΣ

ὁ δράκων δὲ πρὸς τί;

ΔΗΜΟΣΘΕΝΗΣ

τοῦτο περιφανέστατον.
ὁ δράκων γάρ ἐστι μακρὸν ὅ τ' ἀλλᾶς αὖ μακρόν.
εἶθ' αἱματοπώτης ἔσθ' ὅ τ' ἀλλᾶς χὠ δράκων·
τὸν οὖν δράκοντά φησι τὸν βυρσαίετον
ἤδη κρατήσειν, αἴ κε μὴ θαλφθῇ λόγοις.

ΑΛΛΑΝΤΟΠΩΛΗΣ

τὰ μὲν λόγι' αἰκάλλει με· θαυμάζω δ' ὅπως
τὸν δῆμον οἷός τ' ἐπιτροπεύειν εἴμ' ἐγώ.

ΔΗΜΟΣΘΕΝΗΣ

φαυλότατον ἔργον· ταῦθ' ἅπερ ποιεῖς ποίει·
τάραττε καὶ χόρδευ' ὁμοῦ τὰ πράγματα
ἅπαντα, καὶ τὸν δῆμον ἀεὶ προσποιοῦ
ὑπογλυκαίνων ῥηματίοις μαγειρικοῖς.
τὰ δ' ἄλλα σοι πρόσεστι δημαγωγικά,
φωνὴ μιαρά, γέγονας κακῶς, ἀγοραῖος εἶ·
ἔχεις ἅπαντα πρὸς πολιτείαν ἃ δεῖ·
χρησμοί τε συμβαίνουσι καὶ τὸ Πυθικόν.
ἀλλὰ στεφανοῦ καὶ σπένδε τῷ Κοαλέμῳ·
χὤπως ἀμυνεῖ τὸν ἄνδρα.

ΑΛΛΑΝΤΟΠΩΛΗΣ

καὶ τίς ξύμμαχος
γενήσεταί μοι; καὶ γὰρ οἵ τε πλούσιοι
δεδίασιν αὐτὸν ὅ τε πένης βδύλλει λεώς.

DEMOSTHENES

What those words mean is clear.
He seizes things in crooked hands, like claws,
and confiscates them.

SAUSAGE SELLER

What about the serpent?

DEMOSTHENES

That's obvious. The serpent is elongated,
as is the sausage, which is also long.
And sausages, like serpents, suck up blood.
Hence, it says the serpent will now conquer
the eagle tanner, unless the snake's resolve
is broken down by words.[25]

SAUSAGE SELLER

Well, this oracle
makes me sound good. Still, I'm wondering
how I'll be capable of ruling people.

DEMOSTHENES

That's ridiculously easy. Keep doing
what you're doing. Make a complete hash
of public business, mix things together
like sausage meat, and always win people
to your side with well-cooked little phrases
to sweeten them. The other qualities
a leader of the public really needs
you have already—a disgusting voice
and disreputable birth—and what's more,
you're a product of the marketplace.
You possess all the qualities essential
for politics. The oracles agree,
including Apollo's shrine at Delphi.
So crown yourself with a garland wreath,
make a libation to the god of idiots,
and then give that man what he deserves.

SAUSAGE SELLER

Who is going to help me out? Rich men fear him,
and poor men are so terrified they fart.

ΔΗΜΟΣΘΕΝΗΣ

ἀλλ' εἰσὶν ἱππῆς ἄνδρες ἀγαθοὶ χίλιοι
μισοῦντες αὐτόν, οἳ βοηθήσουσί σοι,
καὶ τῶν πολιτῶν οἱ καλοί τε κἀγαθοί,
καὶ τῶν θεατῶν ὅστις ἐστὶ δεξιός,
κἀγὼ μετ' αὐτῶν χὠ θεὸς ξυλλήψεται.
καὶ μὴ δέδιθ'· οὐ γάρ ἐστιν ἐξῃκασμένος,
ὑπὸ τοῦ δέους γὰρ αὐτὸν οὐδεὶς ἤθελεν
τῶν σκευοποιῶν εἰκάσαι. πάντως γε μὴν
γνωσθήσεται· τὸ γὰρ θέατρον δεξιόν.

ΝΙΚΙΑΣ

οἴμοι κακοδαίμων ὁ Παφλαγὼν ἐξέρχεται.

ΠΑΦΛΑΓΩΝΝ

οὔτοι μὰ τοὺς δώδεκα θεοὺς χαιρήσετον,
ὁτιὴ 'πὶ τῷ δήμῳ ξυνόμνυτον πάλαι.
τουτὶ τί δρᾷ τὸ Χαλκιδικὸν ποτήριον;
οὐκ ἔσθ' ὅπως οὐ Χαλκιδέας ἀφίστατον.
ἀπολεῖσθον ἀποθανεῖσθον ὦ μιαρωτάτω.

ΔΗΜΟΣΘΕΝΗΣ

οὗτος τί φεύγεις; οὐ μενεῖς; ὦ γεννάδα
ἀλλαντοπῶλα μὴ προδῷς τὰ πράγματα.
ἄνδρες ἱππῆς παραγένεσθε· νῦν ὁ καιρός. ὦ Σίμων,
ὦ Παναίτι' οὐκ ἐλᾶτε πρὸς τὸ δεξιὸν κέρας;
ἄνδρες ἐγγύς. ἀλλ' ἀμύνου κἀπαναστρέφου πάλιν.
ὁ κονιορτὸς δῆλος αὐτῶν ὡς ὁμοῦ προσκειμένων.
ἀλλ' ἀμύνου καὶ δίωκε καὶ τροπὴν αὐτοῦ ποιοῦ.

DEMOSTHENES

But there are a thousand excellent men,
the Knights, who hate him. They will assist you—
along with the upright and honest men
among the citizens, all people here
in this audience who have any brains,
and me. The god will help you out as well.
Have no fear. You won't see a face like his—
the men who make the masks were just too scared
to dare prepare something that looked like him.
Still he'll be easy enough to recognize.
This audience is smart enough for that![26]

NICIAS *[from inside]*

What the hell! The Paphlagonian—
he's coming out! We're done for!

[The Paphlagonian rushes out of the house.]

PAPHLAGONIAN *[roaring]*

By the twelve gods, you won't get away with this—
an ongoing conspiracy against the public!
What going on with this Chalcidian cup?
You must be stirring an insurgency
among Chalcidians. You will be killed—
you pair of polluted rogues—you will perish![27]

[The Sausage Seller backs away in terror.]

DEMOSTHENES *[to the Sausage Seller]*

Hey, why are you backing off? Stand up to him!
O noble sausage seller, do not betray
our public cause!

[Demosthenes starts shouting at the Chorus offstage in the wings.]

You Knights, cavalry men,
help us out—now is a time of crisis!
Simon, Panaetius! Charge the right wing!

[He goes to the Sausage Seller and turns him to face the Paphlagonian.]

They're getting close. Come on, defend yourself!
Wheel round for an attack! Their cloud of dust
is clearly visible. They're coming on—
almost here. So fight back! Chase him away!
Get that Paphlagonian out of here!

ΧΟΡΟΣ

παῖε παῖε τὸν πανοῦργον καὶ ταραξιππόστρατον
καὶ τελώνην καὶ φάραγγα καὶ Χάρυβδιν ἁρπαγῆς,
καὶ πανοῦργον καὶ πανοῦργον· πολλάκις γὰρ αὔτ᾽ ἐρῶ.
καὶ γὰρ οὗτος ἦν πανοῦργος πολλάκις τῆς ἡμέρας.
ἀλλὰ παῖε καὶ δίωκε καὶ τάραττε καὶ κύκα
καὶ βδελύττου, καὶ γὰρ ἡμεῖς, κἀπικείμενος βόα·
εὐλαβοῦ δὲ μὴ ᾽κφύγῃ σε· καὶ γὰρ οἶδε τὰς ὁδούς,
ἅσπερ Εὐκράτης ἔφευγεν εὐθὺ τῶν κυρηβίων.

ΠΑΦΛΑΓΩΝΝ

ὦ γέροντες ἡλιασταί, φράτερες τριωβόλου,
οὓς ἐγὼ βόσκω κεκραγὼς καὶ δίκαια κἄδικα,
παραβοηθεῖθ᾽, ὡς ὑπ᾽ ἀνδρῶν τύπτομαι ξυνωμοτῶν.

ΧΟΡΟΣ

ἐν δίκῃ γ᾽, ἐπεὶ τὰ κοινὰ πρὶν λαχεῖν κατεσθίεις,
κἀποσυκάζεις πιέζων τοὺς ὑπευθύνους σκοπῶν,
ὅστις αὐτῶν ὠμός ἐστιν ἢ πέπων ἢ μὴ πέπων,
κἄν τιν᾽ αὐτῶν γνῷς ἀπράγμον᾽ ὄντα καὶ κεχηνότα,
καταγαγὼν ἐκ Χερρονήσου διαβαλὼν ἀγκυρίσας
εἶτ᾽ ἀποστρέψας τὸν ὦμον αὐτὸν ἐνεκολήβασας·
καὶ σκοπεῖς γε τῶν πολιτῶν ὅστις ἐστὶν ἀμνοκῶν,
πλούσιος καὶ μὴ πονηρὸς καὶ τρέμων τὰ πράγματα.

ΠΑΦΛΑΓΩΝΝ

ξυνεπίκεισθ᾽ ὑμεῖς; ἐγὼ δ᾽ ἄνδρες δι᾽ ὑμᾶς τύπτομαι,
ὅτι λέγειν γνώμην ἔμελλον ὡς δίκαιον ἐν πόλει
ἑστάναι μνημεῖον ὑμῶν ἐστιν ἀνδρείας χάριν.

[Demosthenes pushes the Sausage Seller towards the Paphlagonian as the Chorus of Knights comes running in. They chase the Paphlagonian around the stage.]

Chorus Leader

Hit him! Hit that wretch who spreads confusion
among the cavalry! That tax collector!
That gaping gulf of greed! That Charybdis![28]
Villain, villain, villain—I'll say that word
again and again, for he's a villain
many times a day! Beat him! Chase him off!
Keep after him! Don't give him any peace!
Show you hate that man as much as we do,
and shout out as you swarm all over him!
Take care he doesn't get away from you.
He knows the alleyways Eucrates took
to scurry off back to the marketplace.[29]

Paphlagonian *[addressing the audience]*

You old jurymen, my three-obol brothers,
whom I nourish with my raucous shouting
of just and unjust things, help me out now!
I'm being lambasted by conspirators.

Chorus Leader

And justly so! Because you gobble up
public funds before you're picked for office,
and when state officers submit accounts,
you squeeze them, as if you were picking figs
to see which ones are green and hard, or ripe,
or not yet fully seasoned.[30] And what's more,
you keep your eye peeled for any citizen
who's stupid as a sheep but has money
and who's terrified of public business,
and if you find one, some simple fool
who avoids all politics, you haul him back
from the Chersonese, then wrap him up
in slanders, hook his knees, twist his shoulder,
fall all over him, and swallow him up.[31]

Paphlagonian

You're attacking me as well? But, my good men,
it's because of you I'm being beaten up—
I was just on the point of proposing
we ought to set up a memorial
to your bravery here in the city.

Χορος

ὡς δ' ἀλαζών, ὡς δὲ μάσθλης· εἶδες οἷ' ὑπέρχεται
ὡσπερεὶ γέροντας ἡμᾶς καὶ κοβαλικεύεται;
ἀλλ' ἐὰν ταύτῃ γε νικᾷ, ταυτῃὶ πεπλήξεται·
ἢν δ' ὑπεκκλίνῃ γε δευρί, τὸ σκέλος κυρηβάσει.

Παφλαγωνν

ὦ πόλις καὶ δῆμ' ὑφ' οἵων θηρίων γαστρίζομαι.

Χορος

καὶ κέκραγας, ὥσπερ ἀεὶ τὴν πόλιν καταστρέφει;

Παφλαγωνν

ἀλλ' ἐγώ σε τῇ βοῇ ταύτῃ γε πρῶτα τρέψομαι.

Χορος

ἀλλ' ἐὰν μέντοι γε νικᾷς τῇ βοῇ, τήνελλος εἶ·
ἢν δ' ἀναιδείᾳ παρέλθῃ σ', ἡμέτερος ὁ πυραμοῦς.

Παφλαγωνν

τουτονὶ τὸν ἄνδρ' ἐγὼ 'νδείκνυμι, καὶ φήμ' ἐξάγειν
ταῖσι Πελοποννησίων τριήρεσι ζωμεύματα.

Αλλαντοπωλης

ναὶ μὰ Δία κἄγωγε τοῦτον, ὅτι κενῇ τῇ κοιλίᾳ
ἐσδραμὼν ἐς τὸ πρυτανεῖον, εἶτα πάλιν ἐκθεῖ πλέᾳ.

Δημοσθενης

νὴ Δί' ἐξάγων γε τἀπόρρηθ', ἅμ' ἄρτον καὶ κρέας
καὶ τέμαχος, οὗ Περικλέης οὐκ ἠξιώθη πώποτε.

[The Chorus has moved to surround the Paphlagonian.]

Chorus Leader *[threatening the Paphlagonian with his fist]*
O you impostor! You slippery rogue!
See how he sweet talks and swindles us,
as if we were senile old men? But if
he jumps this way, I'll thump him with this fist.
If he slips down here my legs will kick him.

Paphlagonian *[appealing to the audience]*
O you people! O city! Look at this—
savage beasts are pummelling my belly.

[Demosthenes pushes the Sausage Seller into the crowd surrounding the Paphlagonian.]

Sausage Seller
Ah, are you now rabble-rousing, the way
you always do when bullying the city?[32]

Paphlagonian
With this loud voice of mine I'll make a start
by forcing you to run away.

Chorus Leader
If your shouting
defeats him, then bully for you—you win.
But if his shamelessness surpasses yours,
then the victory cake belongs to us.[33]

Paphlagonian *[pointing to the Sausage Seller]*
I denounce this man. I claim he smuggles soup
out to the Peloponnesian warships!

Sausage Seller
And I, by god, am accusing this man
of running into the Prytaneum
with an empty stomach, then coming out
with his guts crammed full.

Demosthenes
That's right, by god.
And he carries off prohibited stuff—
bread, meat, slices of fried fish. The people
never considered Pericles worthy
of that honour.[34]

ΠΑΦΛΑΓΩΝΝ

ἀποθανεῖσθον αὐτίκα μάλα.

ΑΛΛΑΝΤΟΠΩΛΗΣ

τριπλάσιον κεκράξομαί σου.

ΠΑΦΛΑΓΩΝΝ

καταβοήσομαι βοῶν σε.

ΑΛΛΑΝΤΟΠΩΛΗΣ

κατακεκράξομαί σε κράζων.

ΠΑΦΛΑΓΩΝΝ

διαβαλῶ σ' ἐὰν στρατηγῇς.

ΑΛΛΑΝΤΟΠΩΛΗΣ

κυνοκοπήσω σου τὸ νῶτον.

ΠΑΦΛΑΓΩΝΝ

περιελῶ σ' ἀλαζονείαις.

ΑΛΛΑΝΤΟΠΩΛΗΣ

ὑποτεμοῦμαι τὰς ὁδούς σου.

ΠΑΦΛΑΓΩΝΝ

βλέψον ἔς μ' ἀσκαρδάμυκτος.

ΑΛΛΑΝΤΟΠΩΛΗΣ

ἐν ἀγορᾷ κἀγὼ τέθραμμαι.

ΠΑΦΛΑΓΩΝΝ

διαφορήσω σ' εἴ τι γρύξει.

ΑΛΛΑΝΤΟΠΩΛΗΣ

κοπροφορήσω σ' εἰ λαλήσεις.

[The Paphlagonian and the Sausage Seller now get into a shouting match.]

Paphlagonian

The two of you will die—
right on the spot!

Sausage Seller

I'll keep on screaming out
three times as loud as you!

Paphlagonian

I'll yell so loud
I'll drown out your noise!

Sausage Seller

And when I bellow,
your hollering will cease.

Paphlagonian

If you become
a general, I'll smear your name with dirt.

Sausage Seller

I'll thrash your back, as if you were a dog.

Paphlagonian

I'll skin you alive with false accusations.

Sausage Seller

I'll use illegal ways to block your path.

Paphlagonian

Look me right in the eye. Try not to blink.

[The Paphlagonian and the Sausage Seller are now engaged in a stare-down contest with very little distance between them.]

Sausage Seller

I, too, was brought up in the marketplace.[35]

Paphlagonian

If you make a sound, I'll tear you apart.

Sausage Seller

Say a word and I'll stuff your mouth with shit.

ΠΑΦΛΑΓΩΝΝ

ὁμολογῶ κλέπτειν· σὺ δ᾽ οὐχί.

ΑΛΛΑΝΤΟΠΩΛΗΣ

νὴ τὸν Ἑρμῆν τὸν ἀγοραῖον,
κἀπιορκῶ γε βλεπόντων.

ΠΑΦΛΑΓΩΝΝ

ἀλλότρια τοίνυν σοφίζει,
καὶ φανῶ σε τοῖς πρυτάνεσιν
ἀδεκατεύτους τῶν θεῶν ἱερὰς
ἔχοντα κοιλίας.

ΧΟΡΟΣ

ὦ μιαρὲ καὶ βδελυρὲ † καὶ κεκράκτα †, τοῦ σοῦ θράσους
πᾶσα μὲν γῆ πλέα, πᾶσα δ᾽ ἐκκλησία, καὶ τέλη
καὶ γραφαὶ καὶ δικαστήρι᾽, ὦ βορβοροτάραξι καὶ
τὴν πόλιν ἅπασαν ἡμῶν ἀνατετυρβακώς,
ὅστις ἡμῶν τὰς Ἀθήνας ἐκκεκώφωκας βοῶν,
κἀπὸ τῶν πετρῶν ἄνωθεν τοὺς φόρους θυννοσκοπῶν.

ΠΑΦΛΑΓΩΝΝ

οἶδ᾽ ἐγὼ τὸ πρᾶγμα τοῦθ᾽ ὅθεν πάλαι καττύεται.

ΑΛΛΑΝΤΟΠΩΛΗΣ

εἰ δὲ μὴ σύ γ᾽ οἶσθα κάττυμ᾽, οὐδ᾽ ἐγὼ χορδεύματα,
ὅστις ὑποτέμνων ἐπώλεις δέρμα μοχθηροῦ βοὸς
τοῖς ἀγροίκοισιν πανούργως, ὥστε φαίνεσθαι παχύ,
καὶ πρὶν ἡμέραν φορῆσαι μεῖζον ἦν δυοῖν δοχμαῖν.

[Pause as they try to stare each other down. The Paphlagonian is the first to look away, straighten up, and continue.]

PAPHLAGONIAN

I admit I'm a thief. You don't do that.

SAUSAGE SELLER

By Hermes of the marketplace, I do.
And if anybody sees me stealing,
I just lie—perjure myself under oath.

PAPHLAGONIAN

Then you're copying someone else's tricks—
doing what I do! And I denounce you
to the city council for possessing
sacred tripe for which you've paid no taxes.[36]

CHORUS

You're a wretched, disreputable screamer!

[They start a rhythmic chant around the Paphlagonian.]

The whole world is full of your impudent snorts—
all meetings, all taxes, decrees, and the courts
you stir up like mud and disrupt the whole town
and deafen our Athens by shouting us down.
For money from tribute you take careful stock,
like spying out tuna from high on a rock.[37]

PAPHLAGONIAN

I know what's going on here—it's been sliced out
of an old piece of leather.

SAUSAGE SELLER

Well, if you
don't know a thing about cutting leather,
then I know nothing about sausages.
You're the one who used a misleading cut
to slice leather from a crappy ox hide
and cheated country folk by selling it,
so before they'd worn it a single day,
it had stretched and was two palm widths bigger.[38]

ΔΗΜΟΣΘΕΝΗΣ

νὴ Δία κἀμὲ τοῦτ᾽ ἔδρασε ταὐτόν, ὥστε κατάγελων
πάμπολυν τοῖς δημόταισι καὶ φίλοις παρασχεθεῖν·
πρὶν γὰρ εἶναι Περγασῆσιν ἔνεον ἐν ταῖς ἐμβάσιν.

ΧΟΡΟΣ

ἆρα δῆτ᾽ οὐκ ἀπ᾽ ἀρχῆς ἐδήλους ἀναίδειαν,
ἥπερ μόνη προστατεῖ ῥητόρων;
ἧ σὺ πιστεύων ἀμέλγεις τῶν ξένων τοὺς καρπίμους,
πρῶτος ὤν· ὁ δ᾽ Ἱπποδάμου λείβεται θεώμενος.
ἀλλ᾽ ἐφάνη γὰρ ἀνὴρ ἕτερος πολὺ
σοῦ μιαρώτερος, ὥστε με χαίρειν,
ὅς σε παύσει καὶ πάρεισι, δῆλός ἐστιν αὐτόθεν,
πανουργίᾳ τε καὶ θράσει
καὶ κοβαλικεύμασιν.

— ἀλλ᾽ ὦ τραφεὶς ὅθενπέρ εἰσιν ἄνδρες οἵπερ εἰσίν,
νῦν δεῖξον ὡς οὐδὲν λέγει τὸ σωφρόνως τραφῆναι.

ΑΛΛΑΝΤΟΠΩΛΗΣ

καὶ μὴν ἀκούσαθ᾽ οἷός ἐστιν οὑτοσὶ πολίτης.

ΠΑΦΛΑΓΩΝΝ

οὐκ αὖ μ᾽ ἐάσεις;

ΑΛΛΑΝΤΟΠΩΛΗΣ

μὰ Δί᾽ ἐπεὶ κἀγὼ πονηρός εἰμι.

ΔΗΜΟΣΘΕΝΗΣ

ἐὰν δὲ μὴ ταύτῃ γ᾽ ὑπείκῃ, λέγ᾽ ὅτι κἀκ πονηρῶν.

ΠΑΦΛΑΓΩΝΝ

οὐκ αὖ μ᾽ ἐάσεις;

ΑΛΛΑΝΤΟΠΩΛΗΣ

μὰ Δία.

DEMOSTHENES

Yes, by god, he did the same thing to me.
It made me a huge laughing stock to friends
and neighbours. Before I'd reached Pergase,
it was like I was swimming in my sandals.[39]

CHORUS *[continuing their chant]*

And right from the start weren't you shameless as hell,
the single protection for those who speak well?
Relying on your crassness you squeeze money out
from strangers with cash, for you've got all the clout.
Hippodamus' son is watching in tears,
but now someone else I like better appears.[40]
He's more shameless by far, and he will win through—
his impudent swindles will clearly beat you.

CHORUS LEADER *[to the Sausage Seller]*

All right, you who were brought up in that place
where men worthy of the name come from,
show us now how a decent upbringing
doesn't mean a thing.[41]

SAUSAGE SELLER

Well, then you must hear
what sort of citizen this fellow is.

PAPHLAGONIAN

Will you let me speak?

SAUSAGE SELLER

No. Of course, I won't,
because I'm a low life, just like you.

DEMOSTHENES

If he doesn't surrender on that point,
tell him you come from a family of thieves.

PAPHLAGONIAN

Are you going to allow me to speak?

SAUSAGE SELLER

No, by god, I'm not!

ΠΑΦΛΑΓΩΝΝ

ναὶ μὰ Δία.

ΑΛΛΑΝΤΟΠΩΛΗΣ

μὰ τὸν Ποσειδῶ.

ἀλλ' αὐτὸ περὶ τοῦ πρότερος εἰπεῖν πρῶτα διαμαχοῦμαι.

ΠΑΦΛΑΓΩΝΝ

οἴμοι διαρραγήσομαι.

ΑΛΛΑΝΤΟΠΩΛΗΣ

καὶ μὴν ἐγὼ οὐ παρήσω.

ΧΟΡΟΣ

πάρες πάρες πρὸς τῶν θεῶν αὐτῷ διαρραγῆναι.

ΠΑΦΛΑΓΩΝΝ

τῷ καὶ πεποιθὼς ἀξιοῖς ἐμοῦ λέγειν ἔναντα;

ΑΛΛΑΝΤΟΠΩΛΗΣ

ὁτιὴ λέγειν οἷός τε κἀγὼ καὶ καρυκοποιεῖν.

ΠΑΦΛΑΓΩΝΝ

ἰδοὺ λέγειν. καλῶς γ' ἂν οὖν σὺ πρᾶγμα προσπεσόν σοι
ὠμοσπάρακτον παραλαβὼν μεταχειρίσαιο χρηστῶς.
ἀλλ' οἶσθ' ὅπερ πεπονθέναι δοκεῖς; ὅπερ τὸ πλῆθος.
εἴ που δικίδιον εἶπας εὖ κατὰ ξένου μετοίκου,
τὴν νύκτα θρυλῶν καὶ λαλῶν ἐν ταῖς ὁδοῖς σεαυτῷ,
ὕδωρ τε πίνων κἀπιδεικνὺς τοὺς φίλους τ' ἀνιῶν,
ᾤου δυνατὸς εἶναι λέγειν. ὦ μῶρε τῆς ἀνοίας.

ΑΛΛΑΝΤΟΠΩΛΗΣ

τί δαὶ σὺ πίνων τὴν πόλιν πεποίηκας, ὥστε νυνὶ
ὑπὸ σοῦ μονωτάτου κατεγλωττισμένην σιωπᾶν;

Paphlagonian *[getting very angry]*

Yes, by god, you will!

Sausage Seller

No, by Poseidon, I won't. I'll fight first
to see who will speak before the other.

Paphlagonian

Bloody hell! I'm going to explode!

Sausage Seller

No, you're not.
I won't allow it.

Chorus Leader

Let him burst, for god's sake—
let him!

Paphlagonian

And what makes you so confident
you think can confront me face to face?

Sausage Seller

Because I am capable of prattling on
and of cooking up some spicy sauces.

Pahplagonian

So you can speak! Bah! If some business matter—
a ripped-up bloody mess—fell in your lap
and you grabbed it, you'd handle it so well!
O yes, you'd arrange things with such expertise!
You know what I think has happened to you?
Like many others, I suppose you gave
a pretty speech in a petty lawsuit
against some foreign resident.[42] You rehearsed
it all night long and babbled it to yourself
in the streets, slurping water, practising
to friends and irritating them with it.
And now you think you can speak in public.
You fool! You've mad!

Sausage Seller

What have you been drinking?
You've turned the city into a place where you,
all by yourself, shout everybody down
and silence them.

ΠΑΦΛΑΓΩΝΝ

ἐμοὶ γὰρ ἀντέθηκας ἀνθρώπων τίν'; ὅστις εὐθὺς
θύννεια θερμὰ καταφαγών, κᾆτ' ἐπιπιὼν ἀκράτου
οἴνου χοᾶ κασαλβάσω τοὺς ἐν Πύλῳ στρατηγούς.

ΑΛΛΑΝΤΟΠΩΛΗΣ

ἐγὼ δέ γ' ἤνυστρον βοὸς καὶ κοιλίαν ὑείαν
καταβροχθίσας κᾆτ' ἐπιπιὼν τὸν ζωμὸν ἀναπόνιπτος
λαρυγγιῶ τοὺς ῥήτορας καὶ Νικίαν ταράξω.

ΔΗΜΟΣΘΕΝΗΣ

τὰ μὲν ἄλλα μ' ἤρεσας λέγων·. ἓν δ' οὐ προσίεταί με,
τῶν πραγμάτων ὁτιὴ μόνος τὸν ζωμὸν ἐκροφήσει.

ΠΑΦΛΑΓΩΝΝ

ἀλλ' οὐ λάβρακας καταφαγὼν Μιλησίους κλονήσεις.

ΑΛΛΑΝΤΟΠΩΛΗΣ

ἀλλὰ σχελίδας ἐδηδοκὼς ὠνήσομαι μέταλλα.

ΠΑΦΛΑΓΩΝΝ

ἐγὼ δ' ἐπεσπηδῶν γε τὴν βουλὴν βίᾳ κυκήσω.

ΑΛΛΑΝΤΟΠΩΛΗΣ

ἐγὼ δὲ κινήσω γέ σου τὸν πρωκτὸν ἀντὶ φύσκης.

ΠΑΦΛΑΓΩΝΝ

ἐγὼ δέ γ' ἐξέλξω σε τῆς πυγῆς θύραζε κύβδα.

ΔΗΜΟΣΘΕΝΗΣ

νὴ τὸν Ποσειδῶ κἀμέ τἄρ', ἤνπερ γε τοῦτον ἕλκῃς.

Paphlagonian

Can you find any man
to rival me? I'll gobble up slices
of hot tuna and wash that down with wine—
a full jug and unmixed—and after that
I'll bugger those generals at Pylos.

Sausage Seller

I'll swallow a ox stomach and pig tripe
and after that gulp down the sauce, as well—
then without bothering to wash myself
I'll drown the politicians with my shouts
and put Nicias in a tizzy.

Demosthenes

I do like
what you just said, but there is one thing
I'm not happy with—you're going to slurp
all the political gravy by yourself.

Paphlagonian

But you're not going to stuff yourself with sea bass
from Miletus and later blow them off.[43]

Sausage Seller

But I will dine on beef ribs. After that,
I'll buy up leases on some silver mines.[44]

Paphlagonian

I'll use force to jump into the Council—
make them all panic.

Sausage Seller

I'll stuff your arse hole—
just like a sausage skin.

Paphlagonian

I'll force you outside
by your buttocks—head down through the door.

Demosthenes

If you're going to drag him outside, by god,
then you'll have to haul me out there, as well.

ΠΑΦΛΑΓΩΝΝ

οἷόν σε δήσω 'ν τῷ ξύλῳ.

ΑΛΛΑΝΤΟΠΩΛΗΣ

διώξομαί σε δειλίας.

ΠΑΦΛΑΓΩΝΝ

ἡ βύρσα σου θρανεύσεται.

ΑΛΛΑΝΤΟΠΩΛΗΣ

δερῶ σε θύλακον κλοπῆς.

ΠΑΦΛΑΓΩΝΝ

διαπατταλευθήσει χαμαί.

ΑΛΛΑΝΤΟΠΩΛΗΣ

περικόμματ' ἔκ σου σκευάσω.

ΠΑΦΛΑΓΩΝΝ

τὰς βλεφαρίδας σου παρατιλῶ.

ΑΛΛΑΝΤΟΠΩΛΗΣ

τὸν πρηγορεῶνά σοὐκτεμῶ.

ΔΗΜΟΣΘΕΝΗΣ

καὶ νὴ Δί' ἐμβαλόντες αὐτῷ
πάτταλον μαγειρικῶς
ἐς τὸ στόμ', εἶτα δ' ἔνδοθεν
τὴν γλῶτταν ἐξείραντες αὐτοῦ
σκεψόμεσθ' εὖ κἀνδρικῶς
κεχηνότος
τὸν πρωκτὸν εἰ χαλαζᾷ.

ΧΟΡΟΣ

ἦν ἄρα πυρός γ' ἕτερα θερμότερα καὶ λόγων
ἐν πόλει τῶν ἀναιδῶν ἀναιδέστεροι· καὶ τὸ πρᾶγμ'
ἦν ἄρ' οὐ φαῦλον ὧδ' ... ἀλλ' ἔπιθι καὶ στρόβει,
μηδὲν ὀλίγον ποίει. νῦν γὰρ ἔχεται μέσος·

— ὡς ἐὰν νυνὶ μαλάξῃς αὐτὸν ἐν τῇ προσβολῇ,
δειλὸν εὑρήσεις· ἐγὼ γὰρ τοὺς τρόπους ἐπίσταμαι.

PAPHLAGONIAN

How I'll clap you in the stocks!

SAUSAGE SELLER

I'll denounce you
as an bloody coward!

PAPHLAGONIAN

I'll stretch your hide
across my tanning bench.

SAUSAGE SELLER

I'll skin you alive—
turn you into a robber's belly bag.

PAPHLAGONIAN

You'll be pegged down—at full stretch on the ground.

SAUSAGE SELLER

I'll slice you up, grind you into mincemeat.

PAPHLAGONIAN

I'll pluck out your eyelashes.

SAUSAGE SELLER

I'll slice your throat.

DEMOSTHENES

By god, we'll force a peg inside his mouth,
like cooks do with pigs, then tear out his tongue,
and peer down past his gaping jaws to see
if there are any pimples up his ass.[45]

CHORUS

There are things in the city, it's clear from this case,
which are hotter than fire, more full of disgrace
than those scandalous speeches all over the place.
This issue matters—it's not just cheap smut,
so let's go at this man, twist him by his butt—
no room for half measures now we've grabbed his gut.

[The Chorus seizes the Paphlagonian.]

CHORUS LEADER

If you wear him down now with a thrashing,
you'll find he's a coward. I know his style.

ΑΛΛΑΝΤΟΠΩΛΗΣ

ἀλλ᾽ ὅμως οὗτος τοιοῦτος ὢν ἅπαντα τὸν βίον,
κᾆτ᾽ ἀνὴρ ἔδοξεν εἶναι, τἀλλότριον ἀμῶν θέρος.
νῦν δὲ τοὺς στάχυς ἐκείνους, οὓς ἐκεῖθεν ἤγαγεν,
ἐν ξύλῳ δήσας ἀφαύει κἀποδόσθαι βούλεται.

ΠΑΦΛΑΓΩΝΝ

οὐ δέδοιχ᾽ ὑμᾶς, ἕως ἂν ζῇ τὸ βουλευτήριον
καὶ τὸ τοῦ δήμου πρόσωπον μακκοᾷ καθήμενον.

ΧΟΡΟΣ

ὡς δὲ πρὸς πᾶν ἀναιδεύεται κοὐ μεθίστησι
τοῦ χρώματος τοῦ παρεστηκότος.
εἴ σε μὴ μισῶ, γενοίμην ἐν Κρατίνου κῴδιον,
καὶ διδασκοίμην προσᾴδειν Μορσίμου τραγῳδίᾳ.
ὦ περὶ πάντ᾽ ἐπὶ πᾶσί τε πράγμασι
δωροδόκοισιν ἐπ᾽ ἄνθεσιν ἵζων,
εἴθε φαύλως ὥσπερ ηὗρες ἐκβάλοις τὴν ἔνθεσιν.
ᾄσαιμι γὰρ τότ᾽ ἂν μόνον,
'πῖνε πῖν᾽ ἐπὶ συμφοραῖς.'

ΧΟΡΟΣ

τὸν Ἰουλίου τ᾽ ἂν οἴομαι γέροντα πυροπίπην
ἡσθέντ᾽ ἰηπαιωνίσαι καὶ βακχέβακχον ᾆσαι.

ΠΑΦΛΑΓΩΝΝ

οὔτοί μ᾽ ὑπερβαλεῖσθ᾽ ἀναιδείᾳ μὰ τὸν Ποσειδῶ,
ἢ μή ποτ᾽ ἀγοραίου Διὸς σπλάλχνοισι παραγενοίμην.

ΑΛΛΑΝΤΟΠΩΛΗΣ

ἔγωγε νὴ τοὺς κονδύλους οὓς πολλὰ δὴ 'πὶ πολλοῖς
ἠνεσχόμην ἐκ παιδίων, μαχαιρίδων τε πληγάς,

Sausage Seller

He's been that sort of fellow all his life,
but these days he thinks he's a real man
for harvesting someone else's grain crop.
And now he's tied that crop up in prison,
the ears of grain he carried back from there—
he's drying them out and wants to sell them.[46]

Paphlagonian

I'm not afraid of you, not while the Senate
is alive and kicking and the people
just sit around looking like total fools.

Chorus

Whatever happens he has no shame.
His colour always remains the same.
If you're not a fellow that I despise,
let me be spread out under the thighs
of Cratinus as his piss-soaked fleece,
or may I be taught to sing a piece
by Morsimus, some tragical song.[47]
You pest, you're always buzzing along,
searching about all around the town,
wherever you go, and settling down
on bribery blooms. O may you please
vomit mouthfuls of cash with the same ease
you swallowed them down—for then I would sing
"Drink, let us drink—it's such a good thing!"

Chorus Leader

And Ulius, I think, who checks grain, too,
and keeps his eye cruising for lads to screw,
would sing out to Bacchus, "O god, thank you."[48]

Paphlagonian

By Poseidon, you will not outdo me
in shamelessness. If you do, may I never
have any part of those offerings of meat
to Zeus, god of our public meeting place![49]

Sausage Seller

And I swear by the many fists whose thrashings
I've had so often since I was a kid
and by the cuts from butcher's knives, I know

ὑπερβαλεῖσθαί σ᾽ οἴομαι τούτοισιν, ἢ μάτην γ᾽ ἂν
ἀπομαγδαλιὰς σιτούμενος τοσοῦτος ἐκτραφείην.

ΠΑΦΛΑΓΩΝΝ

ἀπομαγδαλιὰς ὥσπερ κύων; ὦ παμπόνηρε πῶς οὖν
κυνὸς βορὰν σιτούμενος μαχεῖ σὺ κυνοκεφάλλῳ;

ΑΛΛΑΝΤΟΠΩΛΗΣ

καὶ νὴ Δί᾽ ἄλλα γ᾽ ἐστί μου κόβαλα παιδὸς ὄντος.
ἐξηπάτων γὰρ τοὺς μαγείρους ἐπιλέγων τοιαυτί·
'σκέψασθε παῖδες· οὐχ ὁρᾶθ᾽; ὥρα νέα, χελιδών.'
οἱ δ᾽ ἔβλεπον, κἀγὼ 'ν τοσούτῳ τῶν κρεῶν ἔκλεπτον.

ΔΗΜΟΣΘΕΝΗΣ

ὦ δεξιώτατον κρέας σοφῶς γε προὐνοήσω·
ὥσπερ ἀκαλήφας ἐσθίων πρὸ χελιδόνων ἔκλεπτες.

ΑΛΛΑΝΤΟΠΩΛΗΣ

καὶ ταῦτα δρῶν ἐλάνθανόν γ᾽· εἰ δ᾽ οὖν ἴδοι τις αὐτῶν,
ἀποκρυπτόμενος ἐς τὼ κοχώνα τοὺς θεοὺς ἀπώμνυν·
ὥστ᾽ εἶπ᾽ ἀνὴρ τῶν ῥητόρων ἰδών με τοῦτο δρῶντα·
'οὐκ ἔσθ᾽ ὅπως ὁ παῖς ὅδ᾽ οὐ τὸν δῆμον ἐπιτροπεύσει.'

ΔΗΜΟΣΘΕΝΗΣ

εὖ γε ξυνέβαλεν αὔτ᾽· ἀτὰρ δῆλόν γ᾽ ἀφ᾽ οὗ ξυνέγνω·
ὁτιὴ 'πιώρκεις θ᾽ ἡρπακὼς καὶ κρέας ὁ πρωκτὸς εἶχεν.

ΠΑΦΛΑΓΩΝΝ

ἐγώ σε παύσω τοῦ θράσους, οἶμαι δὲ μᾶλλον ἄμφω.
ἔξειμι γάρ σοι λαμπρὸς ἤδη καὶ μέγας καθιείς,
ὁμοῦ ταράττων τήν τε γῆν καὶ τὴν θάλατταν εἰκῇ.

in this business I will outperform you.
If not, there'd be no point in being so large
after eating nothing but finger wipes.[50]

PAPHLAGONIAN

You mean bread for wiping hands, just like a dog?
You silly fool, on a diet of dog food
how will you battle a dog-faced baboon?

SAUSAGE SELLER

By god, my youth has taught me other tricks.
I'd swindle the butchers by saying things like,
"Hey lads, take a look. You see that swallow?
Springtime is here!" And when they'd look up,
right then I'd snatch off some of their meat.

DEMOSTHENES

O cleverest of men! You planned that well—
like those who eat nettles, you stole your meat
before the swallows came.[51]

SAUSAGE SELLER

And I did it
without being noticed! If one of them saw,
I'd hide the stuff—shove it in my butt crack
and swear by the gods I'd done nothing wrong.
When some politician saw what I did,
he said, "There's no doubt about it—this child
is someone who will rule the people."

DEMOSTHENES

What he said was right. And it's very clear
what led him to arrive at that opinion—
you could steal, perjure yourself, and shove meat
way up your ass.

PAPHLAGONIAN

I'll stop this man's insolence—
or rather, I'll put an end to both of you.
I'll come at the two of you, sweeping down
with a driving mighty wind, confounding
land and sea into a common chaos.

ΑΛΛΑΝΤΟΠΩΛΗΣ

ἐγὼ δὲ συστείλας γε τοὺς ἀλλᾶντας εἶτ᾽ ἀφήσω
κατὰ κῦμ᾽ ἐμαυτὸν οὔριον, κλάειν σε μακρὰ κελεύσας.

ΔΗΜΟΣΘΕΝΗΣ

κἄγωγ᾽, ἐάν τι παραχαλᾷ, τὴν ἀντλίαν φυλάξω.

ΠΑΦΛΑΓΩΝΝ

οὔτοι μὰ τὴν Δήμητρα καταπροίξει τάλαντα πολλὰ
κλέψας Ἀθηναίων.

ΔΗΜΟΣΘΕΝΗΣ

ἄθρει καὶ τοῦ ποδὸς παρίει·
ὡς οὗτος ἤδη καικίας καὶ συκοφαντίας πνεῖ.

ΑΛΛΑΝΤΟΠΩΛΗΣ

σὲ δ᾽ ἐκ Ποτειδαίας ἔχοντ᾽ εὖ οἶδα δέκα τάλαντα.

ΠΑΦΛΑΓΩΝΝ

τί δῆτα; βούλει τῶν ταλάντων ἓν λαβὼν σιωπᾶν;

ΔΗΜΟΣΘΕΝΗΣ

ἁνὴρ ἂν ἡδέως λάβοι. τοὺς τερθρίους παρίει·
τὸ πνεῦμ᾽ ἔλαττον γίγνεται.

ΠΑΦΛΑΓΩΝΝ

φεύξει γραφὰς ...
ἑκατονταλάντους τέτταρας.

ΑΛΛΑΝΤΟΠΩΛΗΣ

σὺ δ᾽ ἀστρατείας γ᾽ εἴκοσιν,
κλοπῆς δὲ πλεῖν ἢ χιλίας.

ΠΑΦΛΑΓΩΝΝ

ἐκ τῶν ἀλιτηρίων σέ φημι
γεγονέναι τῶν τῆς θεοῦ.

SAUSAGE SELLER

Then I'll haul in the sausages and let
myself sail along before the friendly breeze,
while telling you to wail and howl away.

DEMOSTHENES

I'll watch out for the bilges, just in case
we start to spring a leak.

PAPHLAGONIAN

By Demeter,
you're not going to get away with stealing
so many talents from the Athenians!

DEMOSTHENES *[pretending he's on a ship]*

Keep your eyes peeled! Ease off on the sail rope!
There's a north-east wind starting to blow in
a storm of accusations!

SAUSAGE SELLER

I understand
you took ten talents from Potidaea.[52]

PAPHLAGONIAN

What about it? Would you like one talent
to keep your mouth shut?

[The Paphlagonian offers the Sausage Seller a bag of money.]

DEMOSTHENES *[grabbing the money]*

He'd be happy to!
Slacken the main brace! The wind's easing off.

PAPHLAGONIAN

You'll be charged [with bribery]—four lawsuits—
each one carries a hundred talent fine.[53]

SAUSAGE SELLER

You'll be charged with twenty for skipping out
on military service—and thousands more
for theft.

PAPHLAGONIAN

I claim you are a descendant
of those who carried out a sacrilege
against our goddess.[54]

ΑΛΛΑΝΤΟΠΩΛΗΣ

τὸν πάππον εἶναί φημί σου
τῶν δορυφόρων —

ΠΑΦΛΑΓΩΝΝ

ποίων; φράσον.

ΑΛΛΑΝΤΟΠΩΛΗΣ

τῶν Βυρσίνης τῆς Ἱππίου.

ΠΑΦΛΑΓΩΝΝ

κόβαλος εἶ.

ΑΛΛΑΝΤΟΠΩΛΗΣ

πανοῦργος εἶ.

ΔΗΜΟΣΘΕΝΗΣ

παῖ᾽ ἀνδρικῶς.

ΠΑΦΛΑΓΩΝΝ

ἰοὺ ἰού,
τύπτουσί μ᾽ οἱ ξυνωμόται.

ΔΗΜΟΣΘΕΝΗΣ

παῖ᾽ αὐτὸν ἀνδρειότατα, καὶ
γάστριζε καὶ τοῖς ἐντέροις
καὶ τοῖς κόλοις,
χὤπως κολᾷ τὸν ἄνδρα.

ΧΟΡΟΣ

ὦ γεννικώτατον κρέας ψυχήν τ᾽ ἄριστε πάντων,
καὶ τῇ πόλει σωτὴρ φανεὶς ἡμῖν τε τοῖς πολίταις,
ὡς εὖ τὸν ἄνδρα ποικίλως θ᾽ ὑπῆλθες ἐν λόγοισιν.
πῶς ἄν σ᾽ ἐπαινέσαιμεν οὕτως ὥσπερ ἡδόμεσθα;

Sausage Seller

And your grandfather,
I proclaim, was one of the bodyguards . . .

Paphlagonian

What bodyguards? Tell us.

Sausage Seller

. . . to Bursina,
who was wife of Hippias the tyrant.[55]

Pamphlagonian

You're a total rogue!

Sausage Seller

And you're a scoundrel.

[The Sausage Seller threatens to hit the Paphlagonian with a string of sausages.]

Demosthenes

Hit him! Give him a hefty swipe!

[The Sausage Seller starts hitting the Paphlagonian with his sausages.]

Paphlagonian

Oooowww! That hurts!
These conspirators are assaulting me!

Demosthenes

Hit him as hard as you can! And lash him
on the stomach with your tripe and guts.
Punch him in that paunch of his!

[The Paphlagonian sinks down under the assault by the Sausage Seller.]

Chorus Leader *[to the Sausage Seller]*

You brave heart!
The noblest of all slabs of meat! You show up
as a saviour for our city and for us,
its citizens—how well, how brilliantly
your speeches have demoralized that man.
What praise for you can match the joy we feel?

ΠΑΦΛΑΓΩΝΝ

ταυτὶ μὰ τὴν Δήμητρά μ᾽ οὐκ ἐλάνθανεν
τεκταινόμενα τὰ πράγματ᾽, ἀλλ᾽ ἠπιστάμην
γομφούμεν᾽ αὐτὰ πάντα καὶ κολλώμενα.

ΑΛΛΑΝΤΟΠΩΛΗΣ

οὔκουν μ᾽ ἐν Ἄργει γ᾽ οἷα πράττεις λανθάνει.
πρόφασιν μὲν Ἀργείους φίλους ἡμῖν ποιεῖ,
ἰδίᾳ δ᾽ ἐκεῖ Λακεδαιμονίοις ξυγγίγνεται.

ΔΗΜΟΣΘΕΝΗΣ

οἴμοι σὺ δ᾽ οὐδὲν ἐξ ἁμαξουργοῦ λέγεις;

ΑΛΛΑΝΤΟΠΩΛΗΣ

καὶ ταῦτ᾽ ἐφ᾽ οἷσίν ἐστι συμφυσώμενα
ἐγᾦδ᾽· ἐπὶ γὰρ τοῖς δεδεμένοις χαλκεύεται.

ΔΗΜΟΣΘΕΝΗΣ

εὖ γ᾽ εὖ γε, χάλκευ᾽ ἀντὶ τῶν κολλωμένων.

ΑΛΛΑΝΤΟΠΩΛΗΣ

καὶ ξυγκροτοῦσιν ἄνδρες αὔτ᾽ ἐκεῖθεν αὖ,
καὶ ταῦτά μ᾽ οὔτ᾽ ἀργύριον οὔτε χρυσίον
διδοὺς ἀναπείσεις οὔτε προσπέμπων φίλους,
ὅπως ἐγὼ ταῦτ᾽ οὐκ Ἀθηναίοις φράσω.

ΠΑΦΛΑΓΩΝΝ

ἐγὼ μὲν οὖν αὐτίκα μάλ᾽ ἐς βουλὴν ἰὼν
ὑμῶν ἁπάντων τὰς ξυνωμοσίας ἐρῶ,
καὶ τὰς ξυνόδους τὰς νυκτερινὰς τὰς ἐν πόλει,
καὶ πάνθ᾽ ἃ Μήδοις καὶ βασιλεῖ ξυνόμνυτε,
καὶ τὰκ Βοιωτῶν ταῦτα συντυρούμενα.

ΑΛΛΑΝΤΟΠΩΛΗΣ

πῶς οὖν ὁ τυρὸς ἐν Βοιωτοῖς ὤνιος;

PAPHLAGONIAN *[pulling himself together and getting up]*
By Demeter, I was not unaware
of this conspiracy they were framing
I knew what they were nailing together
and hammering into one—the whole scheme!

SAUSAGE SELLER
And I'm not unaware of what you're doing
in Argos. He pretends he's making Argives
our friends, but he's negotiating there
with Spartans—one of his private deals.[56]

DEMOSTHENES
Come on, aren't you going to use any words
to match his language from the building trades?[57]

SAUSAGE SELLER
And I know why the bellows are blowing—
they're forging something for the prisoners.[58]

DEMOSTHENES
Good! O that's good! His carpentry answered
with phrases from the blacksmith's forge.

SAUSAGE SELLER
                                        There are men
in Sparta hammering at it as well.
But if you offer me gold or silver
or send your friends around, you won't stop me
announcing this to all Athenians.

PAPHLAGONIAN
Well, I'm going to the Council right away
to inform them of the conspiracies
involving all of you—those meetings
you have in the city during the night,
all your secret dealings with the Persians
and their Great King and how you're making hay
with the Boeotians.[59]

SAUSAGE SELLER
                                Ah, hay in Boeotia!
What's the going rate for hay?

ΠΑΦΛΑΓΩΝΝ

ἐγώ σε νὴ τὸν Ἡρακλέα παραστορῶ.

ΧΟΡΟΣ

ἄγε δὴ σὺ τίνα νοῦν ἢ τίνα ψυχὴν ἔχεις;
νυνί γε δείξεις, εἴπερ ἀπεκρύψω τότε
ἐς τὼ κοχώνα τὸ κρέας, ὡς αὐτὸς λέγεις·
θεύσει γὰρ ᾄξας ἐς τὸ βουλευτήριον,
ὡς οὗτος ἐσπεσὼν ἐκεῖσε διαβαλεῖ
ἡμᾶς ἅπαντας καὶ κράγον κεκράξεται.

ΑΛΛΑΝΤΟΠΩΛΗΣ

ἀλλ᾽ εἶμι· πρῶτον δ᾽ ὡς ἔχω τὰς κοιλίας
καὶ τὰς μαχαίρας ἐνθαδὶ καταθήσομαι.

ΔΗΜΟΣΘΕΝΗΣ

ἔχε νυν, ἄλειψον τὸν τράχηλον τουτῳί,
ἵν᾽ ἐξολισθάνειν δύνῃ τὰς διαβολάς.

ΑΛΛΑΝΤΟΠΩΛΗΣ

ἀλλ᾽ εὖ λέγεις καὶ παιδοτριβικῶς ταυταγί.

ΔΗΜΟΣΘΕΝΗΣ

ἔχε νυν, ἐπέγκαψον λαβὼν ταδί.

ΑΛΛΑΝΤΟΠΩΛΗΣ

τί δαί;

ΔΗΜΟΣΘΕΝΗΣ

ἵν᾽ ἄμεινον ὦ τᾶν ἐσκοροδισμένος μάχῃ.
καὶ σπεῦδε ταχέως.

ΑΛΛΑΝΤΟΠΩΛΗΣ

ταῦτα δρῶ.

PAPHLAGONIAN *[exasperated]*
By Hercules,
I'll stretch that hide of yours!

[The Paphlagonian leaves, moving toward the city.]

DEMOSTHENES *[to Sausage Seller]*
Come on now!
What sort of brain and heart do you possess?
Now's the time to show if you really hid
that meat inside your butt crack way back when,
the way you say you did. You've got to dash
to the Council rooms—running all the way.
That man is about to descend on them
and slander every one of us, howling
and kicking up a fuss.

SAUSAGE SELLER
I'm going. But first,
I'll get rid of my tripe and sausages—
I'll leave them here.

DEMOSTHENES
Hang on! Rub some of this grease
on your neck and throat, so you can slide out
from his false charges.

SAUSAGE SELLER
Excellent advice—
spoken like a wrestling master.

DEMOSTHENES *[rubbing meat grease on the Sausage Seller]*
All right.
Now take this and swallow it!

SAUSAGE SELLER
What is it?

DEMOSTHENES
You'll fight better when you're stuffed with garlic.
Hurry up! Get a move on![60]

SAUSAGE SELLER
That's what I'm doing!

Δημοσθενης

μέμνησό νυν
δάκνειν διαβάλλειν, τοὺς λόφους κατεσθίειν,
χὤπως τὰ κάλλαί ἀποφαγὼν ἥξεις πάλιν.

Χορος

ἄλλ' ἴθι χαίρων, καὶ πράξειας
κατὰ νοῦν τὸν ἐμόν, καί σε φυλάττοι
Ζεὺς ἀγοραῖος· καὶ νικήσας
αὖθις ἐκεῖθεν πάλιν ὡς ἡμᾶς
ἔλθοις στεφάνοις κατάπαστος.
ὑμεῖς δ' ἡμῖν προσέχετε τὸν νοῦν
τοῖς ἀναπαίστοις,
ὦ παντοίας ἤδη Μούσης
πειραθέντες καθ' ἑαυτούς.

εἰ μέν τις ἀνὴρ τῶν ἀρχαίων κωμῳδοδιδάσκαλος ἡμᾶς
ἠνάγκαζεν λέξοντας ἔπη πρὸς τὸ θέατρον παραβῆναι,
οὐκ ἂν φαύλως ἔτυχεν τούτου· νῦν δ' ἄξιός ἐσθ' ὁ ποιητής,
ὅτι τοὺς αὐτοὺς ἡμῖν μισεῖ τολμᾷ τε λέγειν τὰ δίκαια,
καὶ γενναίως πρὸς τὸν τυφῶ χωρεῖ καὶ τὴν ἐριώλην.
ἃ δὲ θαυμάζειν ὑμῶν φησιν πολλοὺς αὐτῷ προσιόντας
καὶ βασανίζειν ὡς οὐχὶ πάλαι χορὸν αἰτοίη καθ' ἑαυτόν,
ἡμᾶς ὑμῖν ἐκέλευε φράσαι περὶ τούτου. φησὶ γὰρ ἁνὴρ
οὐχ ὑπ' ἀνοίας τοῦτο πεπονθὼς διατρίβειν, ἀλλὰ νομίζων
κωμῳδοδιδασκαλίαν εἶναι χαλεπώτατον ἔργον ἁπάντων·
πολλῶν γὰρ δὴ πειρασάντων αὐτὴν ὀλίγοις χαρίσασθαι·
ὑμᾶς τε πάλαι διαγιγνώσκων ἐπετείους τὴν φύσιν ὄντας
καὶ τοὺς προτέρους τῶν ποιητῶν ἅμα τῷ γήρᾳ προδιδόντας·
τοῦτο μὲν εἰδὼς ἅπαθε Μάγνης ἅμα ταῖς πολιαῖς κατιούσαις,
ὃς πλεῖστα χορῶν τῶν ἀντιπάλων νίκης ἔστησε τροπαῖα·
πάσας δ' ὑμῖν φωνὰς ἱεὶς καὶ ψάλλων καὶ πτερυγίζων

[The Sausage Seller leaves in the same direction as the Paphlagonian.]

DEMOSTHENES *[shouting after the Sausage Seller]*
Remember now—bite the man, slander him,
eat up his coxcomb. Don't come back here
until you've gobbled his wattles.

CHORUS LEADER *[in the direction of the Sausage Seller]*
Go and good luck!
May you live up to my hopes, and may Zeus
god of our public assembly, protect you,
and may you come back to us in triumph,
adorned with the garlands of victory.

[Demosthenes exits into the house. The Chorus Leader turns to address the audience.]

Now pay attention to our formal verses,
you who have on your own already heard
all the different offerings of the Muse.[61]
If one of the comic playwrights from long ago
had tried to make us step out to this audience
and recite a speech, it would not have been easy
for him to get his way. But today our poet
is worth the effort, because he hates the same men
we despise and dares to speak the truth, charging
courageously against typhoon and hurricane.
He says that many of you have come up to him
astonished that he did not long ago request
a chorus in his own name and questioning him
about it. He has asked us to explain to you
why this has happened.[62] He asserts that it was not
foolishness that prompted his delay but rather
that he considered producing comic drama
the most difficult task of all. Many people try
to court the Comic Muse, but she grants her favours
only to a few. And he has long recognized
that you have a fickle nature—for you betrayed
earlier poets once they grew old. He knows well
what Magnes went through as soon as his hair turned white.[63]
He had hoisted many trophies of victory
over his rivals, and though he had created
every kind of sound for your delight, by singing,

καὶ λυδίζων καὶ ψηνίζων καὶ βαπτόμενος βατραχείοις
οὐκ ἐξήρκεσεν, ἀλλὰ τελευτῶν ἐπὶ γήρως, οὐ γὰρ ἐφ' ἥβης,
ἐξεβλήθη πρεσβύτης ὤν, ὅτι τοῦ σκώπτειν ἀπελείφθη·
εἶτα Κρατίνου μεμνημένος, ὃς πολλῷ ῥεύσας ποτ' ἐπαίνῳ
διὰ τῶν ἀφελῶν πεδίων ἔρρει, καὶ τῆς στάσεως παρασύρων
ἐφόρει τὰς δρῦς καὶ τὰς πλατάνους καὶ τοὺς ἐχθροὺς
προθελύμνους·
ᾆσαι δ' οὐκ ἦν ἐν ξυμποσίῳ πλὴν 'Δωροῖ συκοπέδιλε,'
καὶ 'τέκτονες εὐπαλάμων ὕμνων·' οὕτως ἤνθησεν ἐκεῖνος.
νυνὶ δ' ὑμεῖς αὐτὸν ὁρῶντες παραληροῦντ' οὐκ ἐλεεῖτε,
ἐκπιπτουσῶν τῶν ἠλέκτρων καὶ τοῦ τόνου οὐκέτ' ἐνόντος
τῶν θ' ἁρμονιῶν διαχασκουσῶν· ἀλλὰ γέρων ὢν περιέρρει,
ὥσπερ Κοννᾶς, στέφανον μὲν ἔχων αὖον δίψῃ δ' ἀπολωλώς,
ὃν χρῆν διὰ τὰς προτέρας νίκας πίνειν ἐν τῷ
πρυτανείῳ,
καὶ μὴ ληρεῖν ἀλλὰ θεᾶσθαι λιπαρὸν παρὰ τῷ Διονύσῳ.
οἵας δὲ Κράτης ὀργὰς ὑμῶν ἠνέσχετο καὶ στυφελιγμούς,
ὃς ἀπὸ σμικρᾶς δαπάνης ὑμᾶς ἀριστίζων ἀπέπεμπεν,
ἀπὸ κραμβοτάτου στόματος μάττων ἀστειοτάτας ἐπινοίας·
χοὖτος μέντοι μόνος ἀντήρκει, τοτὲ μὲν πίπτων τοτὲ δ'
οὐχί.
ταῦτ' ὀρρωδῶν διέτριβεν ἀεί, καὶ πρὸς τούτοισιν ἔφασκεν
ἐρέτην χρῆναι πρῶτα γενέσθαι πρὶν πηδαλίοις ἐπιχειρεῖν,
κᾆτ' ἐντεῦθεν πρῳρατεῦσαι καὶ τοὺς ἀνέμους διαθρῆσαι,
κᾆτα κυβερνᾶν αὐτὸν ἑαυτῷ. τούτων οὖν οὕνεκα πάντων,
ὅτι σωφρονικῶς κοὐκ ἀνοήτως ἐσπηδήσας ἐφλυάρει,
αἴρεσθ' αὐτῷ πολὺ τὸ ῥόθιον, παραπέμψατ' ἐφ' ἕνδεκα
κώπαις

θόρυβον χρηστὸν ληναΐτην,
ἵν' ὁ ποιητὴς ἀπίῃ χαίρων
κατὰ νοῦν πράξας,
φαιδρὸς λάμποντι μετώπῳ.

flapping his wings, performing as a Lydian
or a gnat, or smearing himself green as a frog,
that was not enough. In his youth things turned out well,
but at the end, in old age, you hissed him away,
that old man, whose jokes had lost their satiric bite.[64]
After that, our poet brought to mind Cratinus,
who once, flowing on torrents of your approval,
raced through unencumbered plains and, as he sped on,
uprooted oak and plane trees and his rivals, too,
and carried them away.[65] And at drinking parties
the only songs were "O Goddess of Bribery,
with sandals made of figs," and "O you composers
of intricate hymns"—that's how famous he was then.[66]
But look at him now—he's a decrepit old man.
His tuning pegs are gone, his tone has disappeared,
his joints have split apart, yet you don't pity him.
He wanders around in his dotage, like Connas,
wearing a withered garland and dying of thirst.[67]
Given his previous triumphs, he should be drinking
in the Prytaneum, and instead of acting
like an idiot, he should be sitting smartly groomed
with the spectators alongside Dionysus.[68]
Look at how much Crates suffered from your abuse
and anger, a man who used to provide you snacks
for not much money and then send you home again,
coming up with the most elegant conceptions
from his decorous lips.[69] But he kept persisting,
on his own, sometimes with success, sometimes failing.
Fearing such treatment, our poet kept on stalling.
What's more, he would tell himself he should first of all
work the oars before his hand could grip the tiller,
and later he'd watch from the prow to check the winds—
only after that would he be his own pilot.
For all these reasons, he moved with great prudence,
not rushing in like a fool and babbling nonsense.
So raise a cheer for the man, a powerful surge
with all of your fingers, a generous urge
at our feast of Lenaea, so that our poet
leaves here with joy and success and can know it—
his forehead all bright with glistening delight.[70]

— ἵππι᾽ ἄναξ Πόσειδον, ᾧ
χαλκοκρότων ἵππων κτύπος
καὶ χρεμετισμὸς ἁνδάνει
καὶ κυανέμβολοι θοαὶ
μισθοφόροι τριήρεις,
μειρακίων θ᾽ ἅμιλλα λαμ-
πρυνομένων ἐν ἅρμασιν
καὶ βαρυδαιμονούντων,
δεῦρ᾽ ἔλθ᾽ ἐς χορὸν ὦ χρυσοτρίαιν᾽ ὦ
δελφίνων μεδέων Σουνιάρατε,
ὦ Γεραίστιε παῖ Κρόνου,
Φαρμίωνί τε φίλτατ᾽ ἐκ
τῶν ἄλλων τε θεῶν Ἀθηναίοις
πρὸς τὸ παρεστός.

— εὐλογῆσαι βουλόμεσθα τοὺς πατέρας ἡμῶν, ὅτι
ἄνδρες ἦσαν τῆσδε τῆς γῆς ἄξιοι καὶ τοῦ πέπλου,
οἵτινες πεζαῖς μάχαισιν ἔν τε ναυφάρκτῳ στρατῷ
πανταχοῦ νικῶντες ἀεὶ τήνδ᾽ ἐκόσμησαν πόλιν·
οὐ γὰρ οὐδεὶς πώποτ᾽ αὐτῶν τοὺς ἐναντίους ἰδὼν
ἠρίθμησεν, ἀλλ᾽ ὁ θυμὸς εὐθὺς ἦν Ἀμυνίας·
εἰ δέ που πέσοιεν ἐς τὸν ὦμον ἐν μάχῃ τινί,
τοῦτ᾽ ἀπεψήσαντ᾽ ἄν, εἶτ᾽ ἠρνοῦντο μὴ πεπτωκέναι,
ἀλλὰ διεπάλαιον αὖθις. καὶ στρατηγὸς οὐδ᾽ ἂν εἷς
τῶν πρὸ τοῦ σίτησιν ᾔτησ᾽ ἐρόμενος Κλεαίνετον·
νῦν δ᾽ ἐὰν μὴ προεδρίαν φέρωσι καὶ τὰ σιτία,
οὐ μαχεῖσθαί φασιν. ἡμεῖς δ᾽ ἀξιοῦμεν τῇ πόλει
προῖκα γενναίως ἀμύνειν καὶ θεοῖς ἐγχωρίοις.
καὶ πρὸς οὐκ αἰτοῦμεν οὐδὲν πλὴν τοσουτονὶ μόνον·
ἤν ποτ᾽ εἰρήνη γένηται καὶ πόνων παυσώμεθα,
μὴ φθονεῖθ᾽ ἡμῖν κομῶσι μηδ᾽ ἀπεστλεγγισμένοις.

CHORUS

O Poseidon, lord of horses
who rejoices in horses' neighs,
in the clatter of bronze-shod hooves,
in swift triremes with deep-blue prows
transporting tribute on the sea,
in contests where those youthful lads
who seek fame by racing chariots
can suffer catastrophic spills,
come to us here, to your chorus,
O god of the golden trident,
you who watches over dolphins,
who are worshipped at Sunium,
lord of Geraestus, son of Cronos,
dearest favourite of Phormio,
and for Athenians the god
more beloved than all the others,
the one our present crisis needs.[71]

CHORUS LEADER

We wish to sing the praises of our ancestors,
men worthy of this land who deserved to carry
the ceremonial robe.[72] In battles fought on land
or on the sea they were victorious all the time,
wherever they went—they brought our city honour.
And when they viewed their enemies, none of them
ever counted up their number. Instead, their hearts
at once were ready for the fray. If they fell down
on their shoulder in a fight, they wiped off the dust
and denied they'd had a fall. Then they would resume
the fight on once again. No earlier general
would have asked Cleaenetus to serve him dinner
at state expense.[73] But now they say they will not fight
unless they get the privilege of front-row seats
and meals, as well. As for us, we believe we should
nobly guard our city and our country's gods
without being paid. We ask for nothing beyond that,
except this one condition: if peace ever comes
and brings our hard work to an end, you will not mind
if we wear long hair and keep our skin well scrubbed.[74]

— Ὦ πολιοῦχε Παλλάς, ὦ
τῆς ἱερωτάτης ἁπασῶν
πολέμῳ τε καὶ ποιηταῖς
δυνάμει θ᾽ ὑπερφερούσης
μεδέουσα χώρας,
δεῦρ᾽ ἀφικοῦ λαβοῦσα τὴν
ἐν στρατιαῖς τε καὶ μάχαις
ἡμετέραν ξυνεργὸν
Νίκην, ἣ χορικῶν ἐστιν ἑταίρα
τοῖς τ᾽ ἐχθροῖσι μεθ᾽ ἡμῶν στασιάζει.
νῦν οὖν δεῦρο φάνηθι· δεῖ
γὰρ τοῖς ἀνδράσι τοῖσδε πάσῃ
τέχνῃ πορίσαι σε νίκην
εἴπερ ποτὲ καὶ νῦν.

— ἃ ξύνισμεν τοῖσιν ἵπποις, βουλόμεσθ᾽ ἐπαινέσαι.
ἄξιοι δ᾽ εἴσ᾽ εὐλογεῖσθαι· πολλὰ γὰρ δὴ πάγματα
ξυνδιήνεγκαν μεθ᾽ ἡμῶν, ἐσβολάς τε καὶ μάχας.
ἀλλὰ τἀν τῇ μὲν αὐτῶν οὐκ ἄγαν θαυμάζομεν,
ὡς ὅτ᾽ ἐς τὰς ἱππαγωγοὺς εἰσεπήδων ἀνδρικῶς,
πριάμενοι κώθωνας, οἱ δὲ καὶ σκόροδα καὶ κρόμμυα·
εἶτα τὰς κώπας λαβόντες ὥσπερ ἡμεῖς οἱ βροτοὶ
ἐμβαλόντες ἀνεβρύαξαν, 'ἱππαπαῖ, τίς ἐμβαλεῖ;
ληπτέον μᾶλλον. τί δρῶμεν; οὐκ ἐλᾷς ὦ σαμφόρα;'
ἐξεπήδων τ᾽ ἐς Κόρινθον· εἶτα δ᾽ οἱ νεώτεροι
ταῖς ὁπλαῖς ὤρυττον εὐνὰς καὶ μετῇσαν στρώματα·
ἤσθιον δὲ τοὺς παγούρους ἀντὶ ποίας Μηδικῆς,
εἴ τις ἐξέρποι θύραζε κἀκ βυθοῦ θηρώμενοι·
ὥστ᾽ ἔφη Θέωρος εἰπεῖν καρκίνον Κορίνθιον,
'δεινά γ᾽ ὦ Πόσειδον εἰ μήτ᾽ ἐν βυθῷ δυνήσομαι
μήτε γῇ μήτ᾽ ἐν θαλάττῃ διαφυγεῖν τοὺς ἱππέας.'

— ὦ φίλτατ᾽ ἀνδρῶν καὶ νεανικώτατε.
ὅσην ἀπὼν παρέσχες ἡμῖν φροντίδα·
καὶ νῦν ἐπειδὴ σῶς ἐλήλυθας πάλιν,
ἄγγειλον ἡμῖν πῶς τὸ πρᾶγμ᾽ ἠγωνίσω.

CHORUS

O Pallas, guardian of our city,
shielding this most sacred place,
surpassing every land in war,
in poetry, and in her might,
come to us here and bring with you
the one who in campaigns and fights
stands there beside us, Victory,
companion in our choral songs,
who wars with us against our foes.
Now show yourself before us here.
For if there ever was a time
when you must give a victory
by any means to these men here
that moment has arrived.[75]

CHORUS LEADER

We know our horses well and wish to praise them.
They are worthy of our tributes, for along with us
they have endured so many battles and attacks.
But we admire them not so much for these events
as for the time they bravely jumped on board the ships,
once they had purchased drinking cups—and some of them
got garlic, too, and onions.[76] Then they grabbed the oars,
just as we humans do, pulled hard on them, shouting,
"Horses, heave! Who's doing the rowing? Pull back harder!
What are we doing? Hey you, you pedigree nag,
why aren't you rowing?" They disembarked at Corinth.
The youngest then dug resting places with their hooves
and went to bring back blankets. Instead of clover,
they fed themselves on crabs if any scuttled up
onshore, or else they caught them on the ocean floor,
so that Theorus said a Corinthian crab
would cry, "O Poseidon, what a cruel misfortune
if I cannot evade those knights either by land,
or even in the ocean depths, or on the sea."[77]

[The Sausage Seller enters, returning from the city.]

CHORUS LEADER

O dearest and most vigorous of men,
how worried I have been since you've been gone.
Now you're back again safe and sound, tell us
how did you make out in the competition?

ΑΛΛΑΝΤΟΠΩΛΗΣ

τί δ' ἄλλο γ' εἰ μὴ Νικόβουλος ἐγενόμην;

ΧΟΡΟΣ

νῦν ἄρ' ἄξιόν γε πᾶσίν ἐστιν ἐπολολύξαι.
ὦ καλὰ λέγων πολὺ δ' ἀμείνον' ἔτι τῶν λόγων
ἐργασάμεν', εἴθ' ἐπέλθοις
ἅπαντά μοι σαφῶς·
ὡς ἐγώ μοι δοκῶ
κἂν μακρὰν ὁδὸν διελθεῖν
ὥστ' ἀκοῦσαι. πρὸς τάδ' ὦ βέλτιστε
θαρρήσας λέγ', ὡς, ἅπαντες
ἡδόμεσθά σοι.

ΑΛΛΑΝΤΟΠΩΛΗΣ

καὶ μὴν ἀκοῦσαί γ' ἄξιον τῶν πραγμάτων.
εὐθὺς γὰρ αὐτοῦ κατόπιν ἐνθένδ' ἱέμην·
ὁ δ' ἄρ' ἔνδον ἐλασίβροντ' ἀναρρηγνὺς ἔπη
τερατευόμενος ἤρειδε κατὰ τῶν ἱππέων,
κρημνοὺς †ἐρείδων† καὶ ξυνωμότας λέγων
πιθανώταθ'· ἡ βουλὴ δ' ἅπασ' ἀκροωμένη
ἐγένεθ' ὑπ' αὐτοῦ ψευδατραφάξυος πλέα,
κἄβλεψε νᾶπυ καὶ τὰ μέτωπ' ἀνέσπασεν.
κἄγωγ' ὅτε δὴ γ'νων ἐνδεχομένην τοὺς λόγους
καὶ τοῖς φενακισμοῖσιν ἐξαπατωμένην,
'ἄγε δὴ Σκίταλοι καὶ Φένακες,' ἦν δ' ἐγώ,
'Βερέσχεθοί τε καὶ Κόβαλοι καὶ Μόθων,
ἀγορά τ' ἐν ᾗ παῖς ὢν ἐπαιδεύθην ἐγώ,
νῦν μοι φράσος καὶ γλῶτταν εὔπορον δότε
φωνήν τ' ἀναιδῆ.' ταῦτα φροντίζοντί μοι
ἐκ δεξιᾶς ἀπέπαρδε καταπύγων ἀνήρ.

Sausage Seller

The result is this—I've crushed the Council.

Chorus *[chanting]*

Then everyone now
should shout with delight!
You speak very well
but your actions excite
much more than your words.
So come on, lay out
in very clear terms
what you've been about.
I really believe
I'd go a long way
to hear what it is
that you have to say.
My very dear chap,
be brave and tell all—
each one of us gets
such joy from your gall.

Sausage Seller

Well then listen. The story is worth hearing.
I went rushing from here right behind him.
He was inside bursting with verbiage,
hurling his thunder, attacking the Knights
with fantastic stories, mountains of words,
shouting they were conspirators—his speech
was very convincing. The whole Council,
as it listened to his lies, grew spice hot,
with gazes like mustard and eyebrows tense.
When I saw they believed what he was saying
and were falling for his lies and bull crap,
I said, "Come on, spirits of impudence,
you cheats, you boobies, you rogues and rascals,
and the Market, too, where I was brought up
as a child, give me boundless brazenness,
a salesman's chatter, and a shameless voice."
As I was saying this to myself, a man
whose arse hole had been buggered out of shape
let rip a fart to my right, an omen
from the gods for which I gave them thanks.[78]

κἀγὼ προσέκυσα· κᾆτα τῷ πρωκτῷ θενὼν
τὴν κιγκλίδ' ἐξήραξα κἀναχανὼν μέγα
ἀνέκραγον· 'ὦ βουλὴ λόγους ἀγαθοὺς φέρων
εὐαγγελίσασθαι πρῶτον ὑμῖν βούλομαι·
ἐξ οὗ γὰρ ἡμῖν ὁ πόλεμος κατερράγη,
οὐπώποτ' ἀφύας εἶδον ἀξιωτέρας.'
τῶν δ' εὐθέως τὰ πρόσωπα διεγαλήνισεν·
εἶτ' ἐστεφάνουν μ' εὐαγγέλια· κἀγὼ φρασα
αὐτοῖς ἀπόρρητον ποιησάμενος ταχύ,
ἵνα τὰς ἀφύας ὠνοῖντο πολλὰς τοὐβολοῦ,
τῶν δημιουργῶν ξυλλαβεῖν τὰ τρύβλια.
οἱ δ' ἀνεκρότησαν καὶ πρὸς ἔμ' ἐκεχήνεσαν.
ὁ δ' ὑπονοήσας ὁ Παφλαγών, εἰδὼς ἄρα
οἷς ἥδεθ' ἡ βουλὴ μάλιστα ῥήμασιν,
γνώμην ἔλεξεν· 'ἄνδρες, ἤδη μοι δοκεῖ
ἐπὶ συμφοραῖς ἀγαθαῖσιν εἰσηγγελμέναις
εὐαγγέλια θύειν ἑκατὸν βοῦς τῇ θεῷ.'
ἐπένευσεν εἰς ἐκεῖνον ἡ βουλὴ πάλιν.
κἄγωγ' ὅτε δὴ γ'νων τοῖς βολίτοις ἡττημένος,
διακοσίαισι βουσὶν ὑπερηκόντισα,
τῇ δ' Ἀγροτέρᾳ κατὰ χιλιῶν παρῄνεσα
εὐχὴν ποιήσασθαι χιμάρων εἰς αὔριον,
αἱ τριχίδες εἰ γενοίαθ' ἑκατὸν τοὐβολοῦ.
ἐκαραδόκησεν εἰς ἔμ' ἡ βουλὴ πάλιν.
ὁ δὲ ταῦτ' ἀκούσας ἐκπλαγεὶς ἐφληνάφα.
κᾆθ' εἷλκον αὐτὸν οἱ πρυτάνεις χοἰ τοξόται.
οἱ δ' ἐθορύβουν περὶ τῶν ἀφύων ἑστηκότες·
ὁ δ' ἠντεβόλει γ' αὐτοὺς ὀλίγον μεῖναι χρόνον,
'ἵν' ἅτθ' ὁ κῆρυξ ούκ Λακεδαίμονος λέγει
πύθησθ', ἀφῖκται γὰρ περὶ σπονδῶν,' λέγων.

I banged the barrier and knocked it over
with my bum, opened my mouth really wide,
and shouted out, "Members of the Council,
I bring excellent news, and I am keen
you be the first to hear it: since the time
this war broke over us, I've never seen
sardines at a cheaper price."[79] Their faces
immediately relaxed—they were prepared
to crown me for my good news. So I said,
as if I were telling them a secret,
that in order to buy lots of sardines
for just one obol, they should with all speed
confiscate all bowls from pottery shops.
They looked at me with their mouths wide open
and applauded.[80] But the Paphlagonian,
guessing what I was up to and knowing
the kind of talk the Council really loved,
made a propoal, "Gentlemen, I think,
in honour of this wonderful event
which has just been reported, we should now
offer a sacrifice to the goddess—
one hundred oxen for this happy news."
The Council then swung back his way again.
So when I noticed I was being beaten
by his bullshit, I upped the ante on him
by shouting out, "Two hundred oxen!"
And then I recommended they make a vow
to Artemis, offering a thousand goats
the following day if the price of sardines
was a single obol for a hundred fish.
The Council was looking my way once more,
and eagerly. The Paphlagonian,
when he heard what I had said, was stunned—
he started to prattle raving nonsense.
So then the presidents and the archers
began to drag him off.[81] The Council members
stood around babbling on about sardines.
The Paphlagonian kept pleading with them,
saying, "Wait a little, so you can hear
what the Spartan messenger has to say.
He's arrived here with a peace proposal."

οἱ δ᾽ ἐξ ἑνὸς στόματος ἅπαντες ἀνέκραγον·
'νυνὶ περὶ σπονδῶν; ἐπειδή γ᾽ ὦ μέλε
ᾔσθοντο τὰς ἀφύας παρ᾽ ἡμῖν ἀξίας.
οὐ δεόμεθα σπονδῶν· ὁ πόλεμος ἑρπέτω.'
ἐκεκράγεσάν τε τοὺς πρυτάνεις ἀφιέναι·
εἶθ᾽ ὑπερεπήδων τοὺς δρυφάκτους πανταχῇ.
ἐγὼ δὲ τὰ κορίανν᾽ ἐπριάμην ὑποδραμὼν
ἅπαντα τά τε γήτεἰ ὅσ᾽ ἦν ἐν τἀγορᾷ·
ἔπειτα ταῖς ἀφύαις ἐδίδουν ἡδύσματα
ἀποροῦσιν αὐτοῖς προῖκα κἀχαριζόμην.
οἱ δ᾽ ὑπερεπῄνουν ὑπερεπύππαζόν τέ με
ἅπαντες οὕτως ὥστε τὴν βουλὴν ὅλην
ὀβολοῦ κοριάννοις ἀναλαβὼν ἐλήλυθα.

Χορος

πάντα τοι πέπραγας οἷα χρὴ τὸν εὐτυχοῦντα·
ηὗρε δ᾽ ὁ πανοῦργος ἕτερον πολὺ πανουργίαις
μείζοσι κεκασμένον
καὶ δόλοισι ποικίλοις
ῥήμασίν θ᾽ αἱμύλοις.
ἀλλ᾽ ὅπως ἀγωνιεῖ φρόντιζε
τἀπίλοιπ᾽ ἄριστα·
συμμάχους δ᾽ ἡμᾶς ἔχων εὔνους
ἐπίστασαι πάλαι.

But with one voice the Councillors all cried,
"Why sue for a treaty now? My dear fellow,
it's because they've learned our sardines are so cheap.
We don't want treaties! Let the war go on!"
They called for the presidents to adjourn
the assembly and then jumped the railing
in all directions. I snuck off quickly
to buy up all the coriander seed
and onions on sale in the marketplace.
Then I passed them all around free of charge
as seasonings, a gift to Councillors,
who had no spices to put on their fish.
They all sang my praises and lavished me
with their attention. So I won over
all the Council with some coriander—
an obol's worth! Then I came back here.

Chorus

In all of these things
you've been very good,
getting your way
as a lucky man should.
The rascal's now knows
that he's met defeat—
another man beat him
at being a cheat,
a far greater rogue,
with many more tricks,
and intricate lies,
and smooth talk that sticks.
You need to take care
to come off the best
when you fight once again
and are put to the test.
You've known for a while
that we are a friend,
your trustworthy ally
right to the end.

[The Paphlagonian enters, returning from the city.]

ΑΛΛΑΝΤΟΠΩΛΗΣ

καὶ μὴν ὁ Παφλαγὼν οὑτοσὶ προσέρχεται,
ὠθῶν κολόκυμα καὶ ταράττων καὶ κυκῶν,
ὡς δὴ καταπιόμενός με. μορμὼ τοῦ θράσους.

ΠΑΦΛΑΓΩΝΝ

εἰ μή σ᾽ ἀπολέσαιμ᾽, εἴ τι τῶν αὐτῶν ἐμοὶ
ψευδῶν ἐνείη, διαπέσοιμι πανταχῇ.

ΑΛΛΑΝΤΟΠΩΛΗΣ

ἥσθην ἀπειλαῖς, ἐγέλασα ψολοκομπίαις,
ἀπεπυδάρισα μόθωνα, περιεκόκκασα.

ΠΑΦΛΑΓΩΝΝ

οὔτοι μὰ τὴν Δήμητρ᾽, ἐὰν μή σ᾽ ἐκφάγω
ἐκ τῆσδε τῆς γῆς, οὐδέποτε βιώσομαι.

ΑΛΛΑΝΤΟΠΩΛΗΣ

ἢν μὴ κ᾽φάγῃς; ἐγὼ δέ γ᾽, ἢν μή σ᾽ ἐκπίω
κἀπεκροφήσας αὐτὸς ἐπιδιαρραγῶ.

ΠΑΦΛΑΓΩΝΝ

ἀπολῶ σε νὴ τὴν προεδρίαν τὴν ἐκ Πύλου.

ΑΛΛΑΝΤΟΠΩΛΗΣ

ἰδοὺ προεδρίαν· οἷον ὄψομαί σ᾽ ἐγὼ
ἐκ τῆς προεδρίας ἔσχατον θεώμενον.

ΠΑΦΛΑΓΩΝΝ

ἐν τῷ ξύλῳ δήσω σε νὴ τὸν οὐρανόν.

ΑΛΛΑΝΤΟΠΩΛΗΣ

ὡς ὀξύθυμος. φέρε τί σοι δῶ καταφαγεῖν;
ἐπὶ τῷ φάγοις ἥδιστ᾽ ἄν; ἐπὶ βαλλαντίῳ;

SAUSAGE SELLER

Ah ha! Here comes the Paphlagonian,
driving a fearful swell in front of him,
seething and foaming, as if he's ready
to swallow me up. My goodness, he's brash!

PAPHLAGONIAN

If I have any of my old lies left,
I'll wipe you out—otherwise I'm done for,
completely up the creek!

SAUSAGE SELLER

I love your threats!
Your smoke-and-mirror chatter makes me laugh
and dance a horny jig—the chicken dance!

[The Sausage Seller taunts the Paphlagonian by imitating a chicken—flapping his arms, hopping around, and making chicken-like noises.]

PAPHLAGONIAN

By Demeter, if I don't eat you up,
kick you out of here, I'll never survive.

SAUSAGE SELLER

If you don't eat me up? And I won't live,
if I don't drink you down and then explode
with you stuffed in my guts.

PAPHLAGONIAN

I'll destroy you—
I swear that by the privileged seating
I won by my victory at Pylos.

SAUSAGE SELLER

My, my—privileged seating! How I long
to see you tossed from your privileged seat
and sitting in a row right at the back.

PAPHLAGONIAN

By heaven, I'll have you clapped in the stocks!

SAUSAGE SELLER

What a nasty temper! Now, let me see—
what can I give you to eat? What nourishment
would you find truly sweet? Why not this purse?

ΠΑΦΛΑΓΩΝΝ

ἐξαρπάσομαί σου τοῖς ὄνυξι τἄντερα.

ΑΛΛΑΝΤΟΠΩΛΗΣ

ἀπονυχιῶ σου τἀν πρυτανείῳ σιτία.

ΠΑΦΛΑΓΩΝΝ

ἕλξω σε πρὸς τὸν δῆμον, ἵνα δῷς μοι δίκην.

ΑΛΛΑΝΤΟΠΩΛΗΣ

κἀγὼ δέ σ᾽ ἕλξω καὶ διαβαλῶ πλείονα.

ΠΑΦΛΑΓΩΝΝ

ἀλλ᾽ ὦ πόνηρε σοὶ μὲν οὐδὲν πείθεται·
ἐγὼ δ᾽ ἐκείνου καταγελῶ γ᾽ ὅσον θέλω.

ΑΛΛΑΝΤΟΠΩΛΗΣ

ὡς σφόδρα σὺ τὸν δῆμον σεαυτοῦ νενόμικας.

ΠΑΦΛΑΓΩΝΝ

ἐπίσταμαι γὰρ αὐτὸν οἷς ψωμίζεται.

ΑΛΛΑΝΤΟΠΩΛΗΣ

κᾆθ᾽ ὥσπερ αἱ τίτθαι γε σιτίζεις κακῶς.
μασώμενος γὰρ τῷ μὲν ὀλίγον ἐντίθης,
αὐτὸς δ᾽ ἐκείνου τριπλάσιον κατέσπακας.

ΠΑΦΛΑΓΩΝΝ

καὶ νὴ Δί᾽ ὑπό γε δεξιότητος τῆς ἐμῆς
δύναμαι ποιεῖν τὸν δῆμον εὐρὺν καὶ στενόν.

ΑΛΛΑΝΤΟΠΩΛΗΣ

χὠ πρωκτὸς οὑμὸς τουτογὶ σοφίζεται.

ΠΑΦΛΑΓΩΝΝ

οὐκ ὦγάθ᾽ ἐν βουλῇ με δόξεις καθυβρίσαι.
ἴωμεν ἐς τὸν δῆμον.

[The Sausage Seller holds up a purse and jingles the coins in front of the Paphlagonian.]

PAPHLAGONIAN

I'll eviscerate you with my nails!

SAUSAGE SELLER

I'll pare down your Pyrtaneum dinners!

PAPHLAGONIAN

I'll drag you to Demos—I'll have justice
from you!

SAUSAGE SELLER

Then I'll haul you off to him—
I can produce more slanders than you can.

PAPHLAGONIAN

You poor idiot! He won't believe you.
I play around with him just as I wish.

SAUSAGE SELLER

You think of Demos as someone you own.

PAPHLAGONIAN

It's because I know all the finger foods
he likes to nibble.

SAUSAGE SELLER

Yes, but you feed him
like a dishonest nurse—you chew the food,
then give him a small piece, once you've swallowed
three times as much yourself.

PAPHLAGONIAN

Besides, with my skill,
I can make Demos do whatever I want—
I can open him up or close him tight.[82]

SAUSAGE SELLER

Well, I can do that, too—with my arse hole.

PAPHLAGONIAN

Well, my dear fellow, you won't be a man
who's known to have showered me with insults
there in the Council. Let's go to Demos.

ΑΛΛΑΝΤΟΠΩΛΗΣ

οὐδὲν κωλύει·
ἰδοὺ βάδιζε, μηδὲν ἡμᾶς ἰσχέτω.

ΠΑΦΛΑΓΩΝΝ

ὦ Δῆμε δεῦρ᾽ ἔξελθε.

ΑΛΛΑΝΤΟΠΩΛΗΣ

νὴ Δί᾽ ὦ πάτερ
ἔξελθε δῆτ᾽.

ΠΑΦΛΑΓΩΝΝ

ὦ Δημίδιον ὦ φίλτατον
ἔξελθ᾽, ἵν᾽ εἰδῇς οἷα περιυβρίζομαι.

ΔΗΜΟΣ

τίνες οἱ βοῶντες; οὐκ ἄπιτ᾽ ἀπὸ τῆς θύρας;
τὴν εἰρεσιώνην μου κατεσπαράξατε.
τίς ὦ Παφλαγὼν ἀδικεῖ σε;

ΠΑΦΛΑΓΩΝΝ

διὰ σὲ τύπτομαι
ὑπὸ τουτουὶ καὶ τῶν νεανίσκων.

ΔΗΜΟΣ

τιή;

ΠΑΦΛΑΓΩΝΝ

ὁτιὴ φιλῶ σ᾽ ὦ Δῆμ᾽ ἐραστής τ᾽ εἰμὶ σός.

ΔΗΜΟΣ

σὺ δ᾽ εἶ τίς ἐτεόν;

SAUSAGE SELLER

There's nothing to stop us. So come on then.

[The Sausage Seller moves towards the door of the house, beckoning the Paphlagonian over.]

Get moving. We should not just stand here.

[The Sausage Seller and the Paphlagonian move to the door of the house and begin knocking on it.]

PAPHLAGONIAN *[calling into the house through the door]*

Demos!
Come on out here!

SAUSAGE SELLER *[calling into the house]*

Yes, father, for Zeus' sake,
come outside!

PAPHLAGONIAN

Come out, dearest little Demos—
so you can see how I am being abused.

DEMOS *[coming from the house]*

Who's doing all the shouting? Get out of here—
leave my doorway! You've torn this apart,
my harvest wreath.[83]

[Demos recognizes the Paphlagonian.]

Ah, Paphlagonian,
who's being nasty to you?

PAPHLAGONIAN

Because of you
I'm being assaulted by this fellow here
and by these young men.

DEMOS

Why is that?

PAPHLAGONIAN

Because I am your loving friend, Demos,
and am very fond of you.

DEMOS *[to the Sausage Seller]*

And who are you?

ΑΛΛΑΝΤΟΠΩΛΗΣ

ἀντεραστὴς τουτουί,
ἐρῶν πάλαι σου βουλόμενός τέ σ᾽ εὖ ποιεῖν,
ἄλλοι τε πολλοὶ καὶ καλοί τε κἀγαθοί.
ἀλλ᾽ οὐχ οἷοί τ᾽ ἐσμὲν διὰ τουτονί. σὺ γὰρ
ὅμοιος εἶ τοῖς παισὶ τοῖς ἐρωμένοις·
τοὺς μὲν καλούς τε κἀγαθοὺς οὐ προσδέχει,
σαυτὸν δὲ λυχνοπώλαισι καὶ νευρορράφοις
καὶ σκυτοτόμοις καὶ βυρσοπώλαισιν δίδως.·

ΠΑΦΛΑΓΩΝΝ

εὖ γὰρ ποιῶ τὸν δῆμον.

ΑΛΛΑΝΤΟΠΩΛΗΣ

εἰπέ νυν τί δρῶν;

ΠΑΦΛΑΓΩΝΝ

ὅ τι; †τῶν στρατηγῶν ὑποδραμὼν τῶν ἐκ Πύλου, †
πλεύσας ἐκεῖσε, τοὺς Λάκωνας ἤγαγον.

ΑΛΛΑΝΤΟΠΩΛΗΣ

ἐγὼ δὲ περιπατῶν γ᾽ ἀπ᾽ ἐργαστηρίου
ἕψοντος ἑτέρου τὴν χύτραν ὑφειλόμην.

ΠΑΦΛΑΓΩΝΝ

καὶ μὴν ποιήσας αὐτίκα μάλ᾽ ἐκκλησίαν
ὦ Δῆμ᾽ ἵν᾽ εἰδῇς ὁπότερος νῷν ἐστί σοι
εὐνούστερος, διάκρινον, ἵνα τοῦτον φιλῇς.

ΑΛΛΑΝΤΟΠΩΛΗΣ

ναὶ ναὶ διάκρινον δῆτα, πλὴν μὴ ᾽ν τῇ πυκνί.

ΔΗΜΟΣ

οὐκ ἂν καθιζοίμην ἐν ἄλλῳ χωρίῳ.
ἀλλ᾽ ἐς τὸ πρόσθε. χρὴ παρεῖν᾽ ἐς τὴν πύκνα.

Sausage Seller
I am this man's rival. For a long time
I have loved you and wished to help you out—
along with many other fine good people.
But we have not been able to do that,
because of this man here. You're like those lads
who play around with lovers, refusing
worthy, decent men and giving yourself
to lamp dealers, cobblers, shoemakers,
and men who trade in leather.

Paphlagonian
Yes, because
I am good for Demos.

Sausage Seller
All right, tell me
just what do you do for him?

Paphlagonian
What do I do?
When the generals were dithering around,
I sailed in there and then brought those Spartans
back from Pylos.

Sausage Seller
And I, while strolling around,
stole a boiling pot from someone else's shop.

Paplagonian
Demos, summon an assembly right now
to find out which one of the two of us
is more friendly to you. And then decide,
so you can make that man the one you love.

Sausage Seller
Yes, do that. Make a choice. Just don't do it
at the Pnyx.

Demos
I would not sit in judgment
in any other place. So we must move
up there. You must appear before the Pnyx.

[They all move over to a rock on one side of the orchestra. Demos sits down on the rock.]

ΑΛΛΑΝΤΟΠΩΛΗΣ

οἴμοι κακοδαίμων ὡς ἀπόλωλ᾽. ὁ γὰρ γέρων
οἴκοι μὲν ἀνδρῶν ἐστι δεξιώτατος,
ὅταν δ᾽ ἐπὶ ταυτησὶ καθῆται τῆς πέτρας,
κέχηνεν ὥσπερ ἐμποδίζων ἰσχάδας.

ΧΟΡΟΣ

νῦν δή σε πάντα δεῖ κάλων ἐξιέναι σεαυτοῦ,
καὶ λῆμα θούριον φορεῖν καὶ λόγους ἀφύκτους
ὅτοισι τόνδ᾽ ὑπερβαλεῖ. ποικίλος γὰρ ἁνὴρ
κἀκ τῶν ἀμηχάνων πόρους εὐμήχανος πορίζειν.
πρὸς ταῦθ᾽ ὅπως ἔξει πολὺς καὶ λαμπρὸς ἐς τὸν ἄνδρα.

— ἀλλὰ φυλάττου καὶ πρὶν ἐκεῖνον προσκεῖσθαί σοι πρότερος σὺ
τοὺς δελφῖνας μετεωρίζου καὶ τὴν ἄκατον παραβάλλου.

ΠΑΦΛΑΓΩΝΝ

τῇ μὲν δεσποίνῃ Ἀθηναίᾳ τῇ τῆς πόλεως μεδεούσῃ
εὔχομαι, εἰ μὲν περὶ τὸν δῆμον τὸν Ἀθηναίων γεγένημαι
βέλτιστος ἀνὴρ μετὰ Λυσικλέα καὶ Κύνναν καὶ Σαλαβακχώ,
ὥσπερ νυνὶ μηδὲν δράσας δειπνεῖν ἐν πρυτανείῳ·
εἰ δέ σε μισῶ καὶ μὴ περὶ σοῦ μάχομαι μόνος ἀντιβεβηκώς,
ἀπολοίμην καὶ διαπρισθείην κατατμηθείην τε λέπαδνα.

ΑΛΛΑΝΤΟΠΩΛΗΣ

κἄγωγ᾽ ὦ Δῆμ᾽, εἰ μή σε φιλῶ καὶ μὴ στέργω, κατατμηθεὶς
ἑψοίμην ἐν περικομματίοις· κεἰ μὴ τούτοισι πέποιθας,
ἐπὶ ταυτησὶ κατακνησθείην ἐν μυττωτῷ μετὰ τυροῦ,
καὶ τῇ κρεάγρᾳ τῶν ὀρχιπέδων ἑλκοίμην ἐς Κεραμεικόν.

SAUSAGE SELLER *[aside, as they move]*

Bloody hell, I've had now. The old man
is very sensible when he's at home,
but whenever he sits down on that rock
he's a gaping idiot, just like some child
trying to catch figs with its mouth wide open.[84]

CHORUS *[to the Sausage Seller]*

Now you must spread out all your sail—
keep your spirit strong. Do not fail
in argument. Beat down that man.
He's tricky—always with a plan
when he seems done for. So attack
like a raging wind. Don't hold back!

CHORUS LEADER

But take care! Before he closes in on you,
first hoist your lead weights into position,
then run your ship at him along the side.[85]

PAPHLAGONIAN

I pray to lady Athena, who guards
our city, that if I have been the best
at serving the Athenian citizens—
apart from Lysicles and those two sluts
Cynna and Salabaccho—I may dine
in the Prytaneum, as I do now,
though I have not achieved a thing.[86] But if
I hate you, Demos, if I'm not prepared
to fight bravely for you all by myself,
may I be destroyed—sawn in two, cut up
into leather straps for horses' halters.

SAUSAGE SELLER

And if I don't love and value you, Demos,
may I be diced up and boiled as mincemeat.
If you don't believe that, may I be grated
on this very table, chopped up with cheese,
mashed into a paste, may I be dragged off
to Kerameikos by my own meat hook
speared through my balls.[87]

ΠΑΦΛΑΓΩΝΝ

καὶ πῶς ἂν ἐμοῦ μᾶλλόν σε φιλῶν ὦ Δῆμε γένοιτο πολίτης;
ὃς πρῶτα μὲν ἡνίκ' ἐβούλευον σοὶ χρήματα πλεῖστ' ἀπέδειξα
ἐν τῷ κοινῷ, τοὺς μὲν στρεβλῶν τοὺς δ' ἄγχων τοὺς δὲ μεταιτῶν,
οὐ φροντίζων τῶν ἰδιωτῶν οὐδενός, εἰ σοὶ χαριοίμην.

ΑΛΛΑΝΤΟΠΩΛΗΣ

τοῦτο μὲν ὦ Δῆμ' οὐδὲν σεμνόν· κἀγὼ γὰρ τοῦτό σε δράσω.
ἁρπάζων γὰρ τοὺς ἄρτους σοι τοὺς ἀλλοτρίους παραθήσω.
ὡς δ' οὐχὶ φιλεῖ σ' οὐδ' ἔστ' εὔνους, τοῦτ' αὐτό σε πρῶτα διδάξω,
ἀλλ' ἢ διὰ τοῦτ' αὔθ' ὁτιή σου τῆς ἀνθρακιᾶς ἀπολαύει.
σὲ γάρ, ὃς Μήδοισι διεξιφίσω περὶ τῆς χώρας Μαραθῶνι,
καὶ νικήσας ἡμῖν μεγάλως ἐγγλωττοτυπεῖν παρέδωκας,
ἐπὶ ταῖσι πέτραις οὐ φροντίζει σκληρῶς σε καθήμενον οὕτως,
οὐχ ὥσπερ ἐγὼ ῥαψάμενός σοι τουτὶ φέρω. ἀλλ' ἐπαναίρου,
κᾆτα καθίζου μαλακῶς, ἵνα μὴ τρίβῃς τὴν ἐν Σαλαμῖνι.

ΔΗΜΟΣ

ἄνθρωπε τίς εἶ; μῶν ἔκγονος εἶ τῶν Ἁρμοδίου τις ἐκείνων;
τουτό γέ τοί σου τοὔργον ἀληθῶς γενναῖον καὶ φιλόδημον.

ΠΑΦΛΑΓΩΝΝ

ὡς ἀπὸ μικρῶν εὔνους αὐτῷ θωπευματίων γεγένησαι.

PAPHLAGONIAN

Demos, how could there be
a citizen who loves you more than me?
First of all, when I was on the Council,
in the treasury I produced for you
massive sums of money—I had some men
tortured, others throttled, and from others
I asked for a financial split—and I
never worried about private citizens,
if I could make you happy.

SAUSAGE SELLER

Hey, Demos,
there's nothing so wonderful about that.
I'll do that for you, as well. I'll steal bread
from other men and serve it up to you.
This man does not love you, and his feelings
for you are not friendly—except for one thing:
he enjoys warming himself at your fire.
That's the first thing I'll demonstrate to you.
You who took your swords against the Persians
at Marathon to save your native land,
and by winning gave us a chance to shout
such glorious tributes—you're sitting down there
on those hard rocks, and this man doesn't care,
unlike me, for I bring you this cushion,
which I sewed myself. Now, lift yourself up,
and sit down gently so you don't strain
that arse that did so well at Salamis.[88]

[The Sausage Seller helps Demos get up and sit down again on a cushion he has brought with him.]

DEMOS

Who are you? Are you from that fine family
of Harmodius? I must say you've done
a truly noble act—you're a real friend
of the people![89]

PAPHLAGONIAN

Such tiny flatteries
to win him over!

ΑΛΛΑΝΤΟΠΩΛΗΣ

καὶ σὺ γὰρ αὐτὸν πολὺ μικροτέροις τούτων δελεάσμασιν εἷλες.

ΠΑΦΛΑΓΩΝΝ

καὶ μὴν εἴ πού τις ἀνὴρ ἐφάνη τῷ δήμῳ μᾶλλον ἀμύνων
ἢ μᾶλλον ἐμοῦ σε φιλῶν, ἐθέλω περὶ τῆς κεφαλῆς περιδόσθαι.

ΑΛΛΑΝΤΟΠΩΛΗΣ

καὶ πῶς σὺ φιλεῖς, ὃς τοῦτον ὁρῶν οἰκοῦντ' ἐν ταῖς φιδάκναισι
καὶ γυπαρίοις καὶ πυργιδίοις ἔτος ὄγδοον οὐκ ἐλεαίρεις,
ἀλλὰ καθείρξας αὐτὸν βλίττεις; Ἀρχεπτολέμου δὲ φέροντος
τὴν εἰρήνην ἐξεσκέδασας, τὰς πρεσβείας τ' ἀπελαύνεις
ἐκ τῆς πόλεως ῥαθαπυγίζων, αἳ τὰς σπονδὰς προκαλοῦνται.

ΠΑΦΛΑΓΩΝΝ

ἵνα γ' Ἑλλήνων ἄρξῃ πάντων. ἔστι γὰρ ἐν τοῖς λογίοισιν
ὡς τοῦτον δεῖ ποτ' ἐν Ἀρκαδίᾳ πεντώβολον ἡλιάσασθαι,
ἢν ἀναμείνῃ· πάντως δ' αὐτὸν θρέψω γ'ὼ καὶ θεραπεύσω,
ἐξευρίσκων εὖ καὶ μιαρῶς ὁπόθεν τὸ τριώβολον ἕξει.

ΑΛΛΑΝΤΟΠΩΛΗΣ

οὐχ ἵνα γ' ἄρξῃ μὰ Δί' Ἀρκαδίας προνοούμενος, ἀλλ' ἵνα μᾶλλον
σὺ μὲν ἁρπάζῃς καὶ δωροδοκῇς παρὰ τῶν πόλεων, ὁ δὲ δῆμος
ὑπὸ τοῦ πολέμου καὶ τῆς ὁμίχλης ἃ πανουργεῖς μὴ καθορᾷ σου,
ἀλλ' ὑπ' ἀνάγκης ἅμα καὶ χρείας καὶ μισθοῦ πρός σε κεχήνῃ.
ἢν δέ ποτ' εἰς ἀγρὸν οὗτος ἀπελθὼν εἰρηναῖος διατρίψῃ,
καὶ χῖδρα φαγὼν ἀναθαρρήσῃ καὶ στεμφύλῳ ἐς λόγον ἔλθῃ

SAUSAGE SELLER

Well, you got him hooked
with lures much tinier than these!

PAPHLAGONIAN

I'm willing to wager my head and state
that no man has ever shown up who loved
Demos more than I do or who was better
at protecting him.

SAUSAGE SELLER

How could you love him
when for eight years you have seen him living
in casks, crannies, and turrets, yet show him
no pity—instead you keep him locked in
and steal his honey? When Archeptolemus
brought peace proposals, you ripped them to shreds
and drove the embassy bringing terms of peace,
whipping their backsides, out of town.[90]

PAPHLAGONIAN

I did that
so Demos might rule over all the Greeks—
for the oracles declare that one day
he must sit in judgment in Arcadia
at five obols a day, if he bides his time.
At any rate, I will feed and care for him
and use fair and foul means to see to it
that he receives three obols every day.[91]

SAUSAGE SELLER

By god, you're not thinking of how Demos
could rule Arcadia—no—but of how
you can rob and take bribes from our allies
and of how the fog of war will guarantee
Demos doesn't see the crap you're up to,
so in his distress, need, and lack of cash
he'll keep gawping after you. But if he
ever takes off for the countryside and lives
in peace there, regaining his fortitude
by munching wheat cakes and saying hello
to his pressed olives, he will realize

γνώσεται οἵων ἀγαθῶν αὐτὸν τῇ μισθοφορᾷ παρεκόπτου·
εἶθ᾽ ἥξει σοι δριμὺς ἄγροικος κατὰ σοῦ τὴν ψῆφον ἰχνεύων.
ἃ σὺ γιγνώσκων τόνδ᾽ ἐξαπατᾷς καὶ ὀνειροπολεῖς περὶ
σαυτοῦ.

ΠΑΦΛΑΓΩΝΝ

οὔκουν δεινὸν ταυτί σε λέγειν δῆτ᾽ ἔστ᾽ ἐμὲ καὶ διαβάλλειν
πρὸς Ἀθηναίους καὶ τὸν δῆμον, πεποιηκότα πλείονα
χρηστὰ 811
νὴ τὴν Δήμητρα Θεμιστοκλέους πολλῷ περὶ τὴν πόλιν
ἤδη;

ΑΛΛΑΝΤΟΠΩΛΗΣ

ὦ πόλις Ἄργους κλύεθ᾽ οἷα λέγει. σὺ Θεμιστοκλεῖ
ἀντιφερίζεις;
ὃς ἐποίησεν τὴν πόλιν ἡμῶν μεστὴν εὑρὼν ἐπιχειλῆ,
καὶ πρὸς τούτοις ἀριστώσῃ τὸν Πειραιᾶ προσέμαξεν, 815
ἀφελών τ᾽ οὐδὲν τῶν ἀρχαίων ἰχθῦς καινοὺς παρέθηκεν·
σὺ δ᾽ Ἀθηναίους ἐζήτησας μικροπολίτας ἀποφῆναι
διατειχίζων καὶ χρησμῳδῶν, ὁ Θεμιστοκλεῖ ἀντιφερίζων.
κἀκεῖνος μὲν φεύγει τὴν γῆν σὺ δ᾽ Ἀχιλλείων ἀπομάττει.

ΠΑΦΛΑΓΩΝΝ

οὔκουν ταυτὶ δεινὸν ἀκούειν ὦ Δῆμ᾽ ἐστίν μ᾽ ὑπὸ τούτου,
ὁτιή σε φιλῶ;

ΔΗΜΟΣ

παῦ ὦ οὗτος, καὶ μὴ σκέρβολλε πονηρά. 821
πολλοῦ δὲ πολύν με χρόνον καὶ νῦν ἐλελήθης ἐγκρυφιάζων.

how you cheated him of many benefits
with the salary you paid. Then he'll come back
from his farmland an angry man, seeking
a voting pebble to use against you.[92]
You know all this and keep him in the dark,
with deceiving dreams about his future.

PAPHLAGONIAN

Is it not disgraceful that you talk of me
in this manner, falsely accusing me
in front of these Athenians and Demos,
when I have done more good things by far
for Athens than Themistocles ever did.

SAUSAGE SELLER *[declaiming the first sentence in tragic style]*

O city of Argos hearken to the things
of which he speaks!

[He turns his attention to the Paphlagonian.]

You dare compare yourself
with Themistocles? He found our city
partially full and left it overflowing.
What's more, while she was enjoying breakfast
he prepared Piraeus for her to eat
and served up new varieties of fish
without getting rid of all the old ones.
But you keep trying to make Athenians
small-town citizens by constructing walls
that close them in and chanting oracles—
and you compare yourself to Themistocles!
He is sent in exile from the city,
while you wipe fingers on fine barley cake.[93]

PAPHLAGONIAN

O Demos, is it not shameful to hear
things like this about me from this fellow,
all because I love you?

DEMOS *[to the Paphlagonian]*

Just shut up, you!
Stop this foul abuse. For far too long now
you've been getting away with duping me.

Αλλαντοπωλης

μιαρώτατος, ὦ Δημακίδιον, καὶ πλεῖστα πανοῦργα
δεδρακώς,
ὁπόταν χασμᾷ, καὶ τοὺς καυλοὺς
τῶν εὐθυνῶν ἐκκαυλίζων
καταβροχθίζει, κἀμφοῖν χειροῖν
μυστιλᾶται τῶν δημοσίων.

Παφλαγωνν

οὐ χαιρήσεις, ἀλλά σε κλέπτονθ'
αἱρήσω γ'ὼ τρεῖς μυριάδας.

Αλλαντοπωλης

τί θαλαττοκοπεῖς καὶ πλατυγίζεις,
μιαρώτατος ὢν περὶ τὸν δῆμον
τὸν Ἀθηναίων; καί σ' ἐπιδείξω
νὴ τὴν Δήμητρ', ἢ μὴ ζῴην,
δωροδοκήσαντ' ἐκ Μυτιλήνης
πλεῖν ἢ μνᾶς τετταράκοντα.

Χορος

ὦ πᾶσιν ἀνθρώποις φανεὶς μέγιστον ὠφέλημα,
ζηλῶ σε τῆς εὐγλωττίας. εἰ γὰρ ὧδ' ἐποίσεις,
μέγιστος Ἑλλήνων ἔσει, καὶ μόνος καθέξεις
τὰν τῇ πόλει τῶν ξυμμάχων τ' ἄρξεις ἔχων τρίαιναν,
ᾗ πολλὰ χρήματ' ἐργάσει σείων τε καὶ ταράττων.

— καὶ μὴ μεθῇς τὸν ἄνδρ', ἐπειδή σοι λαβὴν δέδωκεν·
κατεργάσει γὰρ ῥᾳδίως πλευρὰς ἔχων τοιαύτας.

Παφλαγωνν

οὐκ ὦγαθοὶ ταῦτ' ἐστί πω ταύτῃ μὰ τὸν Ποσειδῶ.
ἐμοὶ γάρ ἐστ' εἰργασμένον τοιοῦτον ἔργον ὥστε
ἁπαξάπαντας τοὺς ἐμοὺς ἐχθροὺς ἐπιστομίζειν,
ἕως ἂν ᾖ τῶν ἀσπίδων τῶν ἐκ Πύλου τι λοιπόν.

Sausage Seller

My dear little Demos, he's the worst of rogues,
who's carried out all sorts of nasty schemes.
Whenever you are yawning, he taps into
the sap of those who audit the accounts
and slurps it down—he uses both his hands
to scoop up public money.

Paphlagonian

You'll pay for that!
I'll convict you of stealing city cash—
thirty thousand drachmas!

Sausage Seller

Why use your oar
just to make a splash? You've been committing
the most disgraceful things against the people
here in Athens. And I will clearly show,
by Demeter, that you received a bribe
from Mytilene—more than forty minas.[94]
If not, then may I not remain alive.

Chorus

O you who appear the greatest benefactor
for all men, how I envy your persuasive tongue.
If you keep on attacking in this way, you'll be
the greatest of the Greeks, and you, all by yourself,
will govern in the city, control our allies,
and, with a trident in your hand, will shake things up,
and by confusing things make piles and piles of money.[95]

Chorus Leader

Don't let this man slip away, now he's let
you get a grip on him. With lungs like yours
you'll have no trouble overpowering him.

Paphlagonian

Things have not yet gone that far, my good friends,
by Poseidon. For what I have achieved
is marvellous enough to shut the mouths
of my enemies, each and every one,
as long as one of those shields from Pylos
still remains.[96]

Αλλαντοπωλης

ἐπίσχες ἐν ταῖς ἀσπίσιν· λαβὴν γὰρ ἐνδέδωκας.
οὐ γάρ σ᾽ ἐχρῆν, εἴπερ φιλεῖς τὸν δῆμον, ἐκ προνοίας
ταύτας ἐᾶν αὐτοῖσι τοῖς πόρπαξιν ἀνατεθῆναι.
ἀλλ᾽ ἐστὶ τοῦτ᾽ ὦ Δῆμε μηχάνημ᾽, ἵν᾽ ἢν σὺ βούλῃ
τὸν ἄνδρα κολάσαι τουτονί, σοὶ τοῦτο μὴ κ᾽γένηται.
ὁρᾷς γὰρ αὐτῷ στῖφος οἷόν ἐστι βυρσοπωλῶν
νεανιῶν· τούτους δὲ περιοικοῦσι μελιτοπῶλαι
καὶ τυροπῶλαι· τοῦτο δ᾽ εἰς ἕν ἐστι συγκεκυφός,
ὥστ᾽ εἰ σὺ βριμήσαιο καὶ βλέψειας ὀστρακίνδα,
νύκτωρ καθαρπάσαντες ἂν τὰς ἀσπίδας θέοντες
τὰς ἐσβολὰς τῶν ἀλφίτων ἂν καταλάβοιεν ἡμῶν.

Δημος

οἴμοι τάλας· ἔχουσι γὰρ πόρπακας; ὦ πόνηρε
ὅσον με παρεκόπτου χρόνον τοιαῦτα κρουσιδημῶν.

Παφλαγωνν

ὦ δαιμόνιε μὴ τοῦ λέγοντος ἴσθι, μηδ᾽ οἰηθῇς
ἐμοῦ ποθ᾽ εὑρήσειν φίλον βελτίον᾽· ὅστις εἷς ὢν
ἔπαυσα τοὺς ξυνωμότας, καί μ᾽ οὐ λέληθεν οὐδὲν
ἐν τῇ πόλει ξυνιστάμενον, ἀλλ᾽ εὐθέως κέκραγα.

Αλλαντοπωλης

ὅπερ γὰρ οἱ τὰς ἐγχέλεις θηρώμενοι πέπονθας.
ὅταν μὲν ἡ λίμνη καταστῇ, λαμβάνουσιν οὐδέν·
ἐὰν δ᾽ ἄνω τε καὶ κάτω τὸν βόρβορον κυκῶσιν,
αἱροῦσι· καὶ σὺ λαμβάνεις, ἢν τὴν πόλιν ταράττῃς.
ἓν δ᾽ εἰπέ μοι τοσουτονί· σκύτη τοσαῦτα πωλῶν
ἔδωκας ἤδη τουτῳὶ κάττυμα παρὰ σεαυτοῦ
ταῖς ἐμβάσιν φάσκων φιλεῖν;

Δημος

οὐ δῆτα μὰ τὸν Ἀπόλλω.

Sausage Seller

You keep clinging to those shields!
You've given me something to grab hold of.
If you loved the people, then you should not
allow these shields to be hung up on show
with their straps attached. It's a clever scheme,
Demos, so that if you wish to punish him,
you won't be able to. You see how he has
a mob of young leather workers with him.
Close to them live men who sell our honey
and those who deal in cheese. All these men
have put their heads together in one group.
So if you were upset and looked as if
you might play around with broken pottery
and have them ostracized, then late at night
they would all run out and take down those shields,
then seize the entries to our stores of grain.[97]

Demos

That's terrible. Do they still have their straps?
You scoundrel! You've been cheating me too long!
And short changing people!

Paphlagonian

But my dear sir,
don't be the slave of the last word spoken.
And don't think you will ever come across
a better friend than me. I am the one
who put a stop to the conspirators,
and without my having knowledge of it,
no one can start a hostile mutiny.
I shout out who they are immediately.

Sausage Seller

You're like the fishermen who hunt for eels.
In calm waters, they catch nothing at all,
but if they stir up mud, they get a catch.
So you, too, gain something profitable
if you disturb the city. Tell me this—
from all those treated hides you have for sale
have you ever given this Demos here,
who you say you love, soles for his shoes.

Demos

No, by Apollo. He never has.

ΑΛΛΑΝΤΟΠΩΛΗΣ

ἔγνωκας οὖν δῆτ᾽ αὐτὸν οἷός ἐστιν; ἀλλ᾽ ἐγώ σοι
ζεῦγος πριάμενος ἐμβάδων τουτὶ φορεῖν δίδωμι.

ΔΗΜΟΣ

κρίνω σ᾽ ὅσων ἐγᾦδα περὶ τὸν δῆμον ἄνδρ᾽ ἄριστον
εὐνούστατόν τε τῇ πόλει καὶ τοῖσι δακτύλοισιν.

ΠΑΦΛΑΓΩΝΝ

οὐ δεινὸν οὖν δῆτ᾽ ἐμβάδας τοσουτονὶ δύνασθαι,
ἐμοῦ δὲ μὴ μνείαν ἔχειν ὅσων πέπονθας; ὅστις
ἔπαυσα τοὺς βινουμένους, τὸν Γρύττον ἐξαλείψας.

ΑΛΛΑΝΤΟΠΩΛΗΣ

οὔκουν σε δῆτα ταῦτα δεινόν ἐστι πρωκτοτηρεῖν
παῦσαί τε τοὺς βινουμένους; κοὐκ ἔσθ᾽ ὅπως ἐκείνους
οὐχὶ φθονῶν ἔπαυσας, ἵνα μὴ ῥήτορες γένωνται.
τονδὶ δ᾽ ὁρῶν ἄνευ χιτῶνος ὄντα τηλικοῦτον
οὐπώποτ᾽ ἀμφιμασχάλου τὸν Δῆμον ἠξίωσας
χειμῶνος ὄντος· ἀλλ᾽ ἐγώ σοι τουτονὶ δίδωμι.

ΔΗΜΟΣ

τοιουτονὶ Θεμιστοκλῆς οὐπώποτ᾽ ἐπενόησεν.
καίτοι σοφὸν κἀκεῖν᾽ ὁ Πειραιεύς· ἔμοιγε μέντοι
οὐ μεῖζον εἶναι φαίνετ᾽ ἐξεύρημα τοῦ χιτῶνος.

SAUSAGE SELLER

Well then,
do you now see the kind of man he is?
I, on the other hand, bought this pair of shoes,
and I'm giving them to you to wear.

[The Sausage Seller gives Demos a pair of shoes.]

DEMOS *[putting on the shoes]*

Of all men I know, you are, in my view,
the finest where the people are concerned,
the most dedicated to the city—
and to my toes.

PAPHLAGONIAN

Isn't it terrible
a pair of shoes could be so important,
and you can't remember all I've done
on your behalf? I'm the one who stopped
those who screw other men illegally,
by taking Gryttus from the voting rolls.[98]

SAUSAGE SELLER

Surely what is terrible is that you
inspected arse holes and prevented
buggers breaking laws when there's no doubt
you made them stop out of sheer jealousy,
fearing they might turn into politicians.
But you can look at Demos, who's so old,
without a coat, and, even in winter,
you don't think it's proper to offer him
a garment with two sleeves. I, by contrast,
am presenting this to you.

[The Sausage Seller takes off his outer coat or cloak and gives it to Demos. Demos tries it on.]

DEMOS

What a fine idea—
even Themistocles never thought of that!
And although that business with Piraeus
was clever enough, in my opinion
it's not a greater notion than this coat.[99]

ΠΑΦΛΑΓΩΝΝ

οἴμοι τάλας οἵοις πιθηκισμοῖς με περιελαύνεις.

ΑΛΛΑΝΤΟΠΩΛΗΣ

οὔκ, ἀλλ᾽ ὅπερ πίνων ἀνὴρ πέπονθ᾽ ὅταν χεσείῃ,
τοῖσιν τρόποις τοῖς σοῖσιν ὥσπερ βλαυτίοισι χρῶμαι.

ΠΑΦΛΑΓΩΝΝ

ἀλλ᾽ οὐχ ὑπερβαλεῖ με θωπείαις· ἐγὼ γὰρ αὐτὸν
προσαμφιῶ τοδί· σὺ δ᾽ οἴμωζ᾽ ὦ πόνηρ᾽.

ΔΗΜΟΣ

ἰαιβοῖ.
οὐκ ἐς κόρακας ἀποφθερεῖ βύρσης κάκιστον ὄζων;

ΑΛΛΑΝΤΟΠΩΛΗΣ

καὶ τοῦτό γ᾽ ἐπίτηδές σε περιήμπεσχ᾽, ἵνα σ᾽ ἀποπνίξῃ·
καὶ πρότερον ἐπεβούλευσέ σοι. τὸν καυλὸν οἶσθ᾽ ἐκεῖνον
τοῦ σιλφίου τὸν ἄξιον γενόμενον;

ΔΗΜΟΣ

οἶδα μέντοι.

ΑΛΛΑΝΤΟΠΩΛΗΣ

ἐπίτηδες οὗτος αὐτὸν ἔσπευδ᾽ ἄξιον γενέσθαι,
ἵν᾽ ἐσθίοιτ᾽ ὠνούμενοι, κἄπειτ᾽ ἐν ἡλιαίᾳ
βδέοντες ἀλλήλους ἀποκτείνειαν οἱ δικασταί.

ΔΗΜΟΣ

νὴ τὸν Ποσειδῶ καὶ πρὸς ἐμὲ τοῦτ᾽ εἶπ᾽ ἀνὴρ Κόπρειος.

ΑΛΛΑΝΤΟΠΩΛΗΣ

οὐ γὰρ τόθ᾽ ὑμεῖς βδεόμενοι δήπου ᾽γένεσθε πυρροί;

Paphlagonian

My god, what silly tricks you keep using
to attack me!

Sausage Seller

No, I'm simply borrowing
your strategies, in the same way a man
who's been drinking, when he needs a shit,
might help himself to someone else's slippers.[100]

Paphlagonian *[taking off his coat]*

You're not going to outdo me with flattery!
I'll put this over him. You can shove it,
you scoundrel!

[The Paphlagonian tries to place his coat around Demos, who rejects the offer.]

Demos *[struggling against the Paphlagonian]*

Bah! Damn and blast you to hell!
It stinks of leather—totally disgusting!

Sausage Seller

He tried to wrap you in that deliberately
so he could suffocate you. That's the scheme
he worked on you before. You know the time
the cost of silphium stalks was so cheap?[101]

Demos

Yes, I remember that.

Sausage Seller

Well, this man here
made sure the cost was low on purpose,
so people would buy the stuff and eat it,
and then jury men sitting in the courts
would kill each other with their farts.

Demos

By Poseidon,
that's just what a man from Shitsville told me.[102]

Sausage Seller

At that time did you not all turn reddish brown
from all the farting.

ΔΗΜΟΣ

καὶ νὴ Δί᾽ ἦν γε τοῦτο Πυρράνδρου τὸ μηχάνημα.

ΠΑΦΛΑΓΩΝΝ

οἵοισί μ᾽ ὦ πανοῦργε βωμολοχεύμασιν ταράττεις.

ΑΛΛΑΝΤΟΠΩΛΗΣ

ἡ γὰρ θεός μ᾽ ἐκέλευσε νικῆσαί σ᾽ ἀλαζονείαις.

ΠΑΦΛΑΓΩΝΝ

ἀλλ᾽ οὐχὶ νικήσεις. ἐγὼ γάρ φημί σοι παρέξειν
ὦ Δῆμε μηδὲν δρῶντι μισθοῦ τρύβλιον ῥοφῆσαι.

ΑΛΛΑΝΤΟΠΩΛΗΣ

ἐγὼ δὲ κυλίχνιόν γέ σοι καὶ φάρμακον δίδωμι
τἀν τοῖσιν ἀντικνημίοις ἑλκύδρια περιαλείφειν.

ΠΑΦΛΑΓΩΝΝ

ἐγὼ δὲ τὰς πολιάς γέ σοὐκλέγων νέον ποιήσω.

ΑΛΛΑΝΤΟΠΩΛΗΣ

ἰδοὺ δέχου κέρκον λαγὼ τὠφθαλμιδίω περιψῆν.

ΠΑΦΛΑΓΩΝΝ

ἀπομυξάμενος ὦ Δῆμέ μου πρὸς τὴν κεφαλὴν ἀποψῶ.

ΑΛΛΑΝΤΟΠΩΛΗΣ

ἐμοῦ μὲν οὖν.

ΠΑΦΛΑΓΩΝΝ

ἐμοῦ μὲν οὖν.

DEMOS

By god, that was a scheme
worthy of some rogue we caught red handed.[103]

PAPHLAGONIAN *[aside to the Sausage Seller]*

You bastard!
You're pissing me off with all this foolery.

SAUSAGE SELLER

Well, the goddess told me I could beat you
in slinging bullshit.

PAPHLAGONIAN

But you won't prevail.

[He turns back to Demos]

Demos, I say I'll offer you a bowl
of state money, a salary, to feast on—
and you don't ever have to do a thing!

SAUSAGE SELLER

And I'm giving you this small container,
some ointment, to rub over these bruises
on your shins.

PAPHLAGONIAN

But I'll pluck out your grey hairs
and make you young again.

SAUSAGE SELLER

Look here, take this—
a hare's tail to wipe your dear little eyes.

PAPHLAGONIAN *[putting his head in Demos' lap]*

Blow your nose, Demos, and then use my head
to wipe snot from your fingers.

SAUSAGE SELLER *[shoving his head down, too]*

No, no. Use mine.

PAPHLAGONIAN

No, mine!

ἐγώ σε ποιήσω τριηραρχεῖν
ἀναλίσκοντα τῶν
σαυτοῦ, παλαιὰν ναῦν ἔχοντ',
εἰς ἣν ἀναλῶν οὐκ ἐφέξεις
οὐδὲ ναυπηγούμενος·
διαμηχανήσομαί θ' ὅπως
ἂν ἱστίον σαπρὸν λάβῃς.

ΑΛΛΑΝΤΟΠΩΛΗΣ

ἁνὴρ παφλάζει, παῦε παῦ',
ὑπερζέων· ὑφελκτέον
τῶν δᾳδίων ἀπαρυστέον
τε τῶν ἀπειλῶν ταυτῃί.

ΠΑΦΛΑΓΩΝΝ

δώσεις ἐμοὶ καλὴν δίκην
ἰπούμενος ταῖς ἐσφοραῖς.
ἐγὼ γὰρ ἐς τοὺς πλουσίους
σπεύσω σ' ὅπως ἂν ἐγγραφῇς.

ΑΛΛΑΝΤΟΠΩΛΗΣ

ἐγὼ δ' ἀπειλήσω μὲν οὐδέν,
εὔχομαι δέ σοι ταδί·
τὸ μὲν τάγηνον τευθίδων
ἐφεστάναι σίζον· σὲ δὲ
γνώμην ἐρεῖν μέλλοντα περὶ
Μιλησίων καὶ κερδανεῖν
τάλαντον, ἣν κατεργάσῃ,
σπεύδειν ὅπως τῶν τευθίδων
ἐμπλήμενος φθαίης ἔτ' εἰς
ἐκκλησίαν ἐλθών· ἔπειτα
πρὶν φαγεῖν ἀνὴρ μεθήκοι,
καὶ σὺ τὸ τάλαντον λαβεῖν
βουλόμενος ἐσθίων
ἐναποπνιγείης.

[To the Sausage Seller]

I'll make you captain of a ship—
that will take all your money. You'll have
an old ship, so you never see an end
to spending cash and making more repairs.
I'll make sure you get one with rotten sails.[104]

SAUSAGE SELLER *[pretending to be very alarmed]*

The man is on the boil! Stop! That's enough!
He's boiling over. We have to pull away
some of the faggots and skim off his threats
with this ladle.[105]

PAPHLAGONIAN

I'll make you pay for this—
I'll crush you with taxes. I'll make sure your name
is listed among those with lots of cash.[106]

SAUSAGE SELLER

I will make no threats. But I have a wish—
may your saucepan of squid be standing there
sizzling hot and you about to announce
your view of the Milesians and so gain
a talent for yourself if you win out;
may you be making haste to eat the squid
and still get to the meeting in good time,
but before you eat the meal, may a man
come for you, and you, in your eagerness
to get that talent, swallow down the squid
and choke on it.

Χορος

εὖ γε νὴ τὸν Δία καὶ τὸν Ἀπόλλω καὶ τὴν Δήμητρα.

Δημος

κἀμοὶ δοκεῖ· καὶ τἄλλα γ᾽ εἶναι καταφανῶς
ἀγαθὸς πολίτης, οἷος οὐδείς πω χρόνου
ἀνὴρ γεγένηται τοῖσι πολλοῖς τοὐβολοῦ.
σὺ δ᾽ ὦ Παφλαγὼν φάσκων φιλεῖν μ᾽ ἐσκορόδισας.
καὶ νῦν ἀπόδος τὸν δακτύλιον, ὡς οὐκέτι
ἐμοὶ ταμιεύσεις.

Παφλαγωνν

ἔχε· τοσοῦτον δ᾽ ἴσθ᾽ ὅτι,
εἰ μή μ᾽ ἐάσεις ἐπιτροπεύειν, ἕτερος αὖ
ἐμοῦ πανουργότερός τις ἀναφανήσεται.

Δημος

οὐκ ἔσθ᾽ ὅπως ὁ δακτύλιός ἐσθ᾽ οὑτοσὶ
οὑμός· τὸ γοῦν σημεῖον ἕτερον φαίνεται,
ἀλλ᾽ ἢ οὐ καθορῶ.

Αλλαντοπωλης

φέρ᾽ ἴδω τί σοι σημεῖον ἦν;

Δημος

δημοῦ βοείου θρῖον ἐξωπτημένον.

Αλλαντοπωλης

οὐ τοῦτ᾽ ἔνεστιν.

Δημος

οὐ τὸ θρῖον; ἀλλὰ τί;

Αλλαντοπωλης

λάρος κεχηνὼς ἐπὶ πέτρας δημηγορῶν.

Δημος

αἰβοῖ τάλας.

CHORUS LEADER

By Zeus, that's a splendid wish!
Yes, by Apollo and Demeter, too!

DEMOS

I agree, and it's clear enough this man
is a fine citizen. It's been ages
since a man of his sort has come along
for the vulgar common folk. As for you,
Paphlagonian, you say you love me,
but you just make me ready for a fight.
Now, hand back my signet ring—no longer
will you be my steward.

PAPHLAGONIAN *[removing a large ring]*

Take it. But know this—
if you won't allow me to be your steward,
another man will show up and get his turn,
someone more disreputable than me.

DEMOS *[inspecting the ring]*

This cannot be my ring. It looks as if
the seal's been changed, unless I'm going blind.

SAUSAGE SELLER

Let me have a look. What was your seal?

DEMOS

A fig leaf stuffed with beef fat.

SAUSAGE SELLER

That's not what's here.

DEMOS

Not a fig leaf? What is it, then?

SAUSAGE SELLER

A sea gull
with its mouth wide open—making a speech
perched high up on a rock.[107]

DEMOS

O that's dreadful!

ΑΛΛΑΝΤΟΠΩΛΗΣ

τί ἔστιν;

ΔΗΜΟΣ

ἀπόφερ᾽ ἐκποδών.
οὐ τὸν ἐμὸν εἶχεν ἀλλὰ τὸν Κλεωνύμου.
παρ᾽ ἐμοῦ δὲ τουτονὶ λαβὼν ταμίευέ μοι.

ΠΑΦΛΑΓΩΝΝ

μὴ δῆτά πώ γ᾽ ὦ δέσποτ᾽, ἀντιβολῶ σ᾽ ἐγώ,
πρὶν ἄν γε τῶν χρησμῶν ἀκούσῃς τῶν ἐμῶν.

ΑΛΛΑΝΤΟΠΩΛΗΣ

καὶ τῶν ἐμῶν νυν.

ΠΑΦΛΑΓΩΝΝ

ἀλλ᾽ ἐὰν τούτῳ πίθῃ,
μολγὸν γενέσθαι δεῖ σε.

ΑΛΛΑΝΤΟΠΩΛΗΣ

κἄν γε τουτῳί,
ψωλὸν γενέσθαι δεῖ σε μέχρι τοῦ μυρρίνου.

ΠΑΦΛΑΓΩΝΝ

ἀλλ᾽ οἵ γ᾽ ἐμοὶ λέγουσιν ὡς ἄρξαι σε δεῖ
χώρας ἁπάσης ἐστεφανωμένον ῥόδοις.

ΑΛΛΑΝΤΟΠΩΛΗΣ

οὑμοὶ δέ γ᾽ αὖ λέγουσιν ὡς ἁλουργίδα
ἔχων κατάπαστον καὶ στεφάνην ἐφ᾽ ἅρματος
χρυσοῦ διώξει Σμικύθην καὶ κύριον.

ΧΟΡΟΣ

καὶ μὴν ἔνεγκ᾽ αὐτοὺς ἰών, ἵν᾽ οὑτοσὶ
αὐτῶν ἀκούσῃ.

ΔΗΜΟΣ

πάνυ γε.

SAUSAGE SELLER
What's the matter?

DEMOS
Put that ring away!
Out of my sight! It's not my signet ring.
It must belong to that Cleonymus.[108]

[Demos produces another ring.]

I'll give you this one. You can be my steward.

PAPHLAGONIAN
Master, don't do that yet, I implore you.
Not before you've heard my oracles.

SAUSAGE SELLER
And mine, as well.

PAPHLAGONIAN
If you believe this man,
you'll be flayed into a leather bottle.

SAUSAGE SELLER
And if you trust him, your prick will be sliced
and cut down to a twig.

PAPHLAGONIAN
My oracles
state that you are to govern every land
with a crown of roses.

SAUSAGE SELLER
And mine predict
you will wear an embroidered purple robe
with a crown and, standing in a gold chariot
you'll pursue Smicythos and his husband
in the courts.[109]

CHORUS LEADER *[to Sausage Seller]*
Well then, get the oracles,
so that Demos here can listen to them.

SAUSAGE SELLER
All right.

ΧΟΡΟΣ

καὶ σύ νυν φέρε.

ΠΑΦΛΑΓΩΝΝ

ἰδού.

ΑΛΛΑΝΤΟΠΩΛΗΣ

ἰδοὺ νὴ τὸν Δί᾽· οὐδὲν κωλύει.

ΧΟΡΟΣ

ἥδιστον φάος ἡμέρας
ἔσται τοῖσι παροῦσι καὶ
τοῖσι δεῦρ᾽ ἀφικνουμένοις,
ἢν Κλέων ἀπόληται.
καίτοι πρεσβυτέρων τινῶν
οἵων ἀργαλεωτάτων
ἐν τῷ δείγματι τῶν δικῶν
ἤκουσ᾽ ἀντιλεγόντων,
ὡς εἰ μὴ ᾽γένεθ᾽ οὗτος ἐν
τῇ πόλει μέγας, οὐκ ἂν ἤστην
σκεύη δύο χρησίμω,
δοῖδυξ οὐδὲ τορύνη.
ἀλλὰ καὶ τόδ᾽ ἔγωγε θαυμάζω
τῆς ὑομουσίας
αὐτοῦ· φασὶ γὰρ αὐτὸν οἱ
παῖδες οἳ ξυνεφοίτων,
τὴν Δωριστὶ μόνην ἂν ἁρμόττεσθαι
θαμὰ τὴν λύραν,
ἄλλην δ᾽ οὐκ ἐθέλειν μαθεῖν·
κᾆτα τὸν κιθαριστὴν
ὀργισθέντ᾽ ἀπάγειν κελεύειν,
ὡς ἁρμονίαν ὁ παῖς
οὗτος οὐ δύναται μαθεῖν
ἢν μὴ Δωροδοκιστί.

ΠΑΦΛΑΓΩΝΝ

ἰδοὺ θέασαι, κοὐχ ἅπαντας ἐκφέρω.

CHORUS LEADER *[to the Paphlagonian]*

And you get yours, as well.

PAPHLAGONIAN

I'll get them.

SAUSAGE SELLER

By god, we'll do it. Nothing's stopping us.

[The Paphlagonian goes into the house to fetch his oracles. The Sausage Seller moves over to his stuff and rummages through it to find some papers that he can pretend are oracles.]

CHORUS

How very sweet will be the light of day
for those who visit here and those who stay
if Cleon is destroyed—though I did hear
some crotchety old geezers speaking near
the list of law suits by the market gate
who claimed if he had not become so great
the city would lack two useful boons
our pounding pestles and our stirring spoons.[110]
I'm amazed in music he is such a swine.
His class mates at school say all the time
he'd tune his strings in the Dorian way,
unwilling to find out how he might play
a different mode.[111] His teacher grew stern
and sent him away, "This boy will not learn.
The Dorian style is all he will play,
and when he does he expects you to pay."[112]

PAPHLAGONIAN *[coming from the house with a pile of scrolls]*

Here, look at this lot. I haven't brought out
all of them.

ΑΛΛΑΝΤΟΠΩΛΗΣ

οἴμ᾽ ὡς χεσείω, κοὐχ ἅπαντας ἐκφέρω.

ΔΗΜΟΣ

ταυτὶ τί ἔστι;

ΠΑΦΛΑΓΩΝΝ

λόγια.

ΔΗΜΟΣ

πάντ᾽;

ΠΑΦΛΑΓΩΝΝ

ἐθαύμασας;
καὶ νὴ Δί᾽ ἔτι γέ μοὔστι κιβωτὸς πλέα.

ΑΛΛΑΝΤΟΠΩΛΗΣ

ἐμοὶ δ᾽ ὑπερῷον καὶ ξυνοικία δύο.

ΔΗΜΟΣ

φέρ᾽ ἴδω, τίνος γάρ εἰσιν οἱ χρησμοί ποτε;

ΠΑΦΛΑΓΩΝΝ

οὑμοὶ μέν εἰσι Βάκιδος.

ΔΗΜΟΣ

οἱ δὲ σοὶ τίνος;

ΑΛΛΑΝΤΟΠΩΛΗΣ

Γλάνιδος, ἀδελφοῦ τοῦ Βάκιδος γεραιτέρου.

ΔΗΜΟΣ

εἰσὶν δὲ περὶ τοῦ;

ΠΑΦΛΑΓΩΝΝ

περὶ Ἀθηνῶν, περὶ Πύλου,
περὶ σοῦ, περὶ ἐμοῦ, περὶ ἁπάντων πραγμάτων.

ΔΗΜΟΣ

οἱ σοὶ δὲ περὶ τοῦ;

Sausage Seller *[with an even bigger pile of scrolls]*
I can't carry all of mine.
By god, I need to take a shit!

Demos
What is this?

Paphlagonian
Oracles.

Demos
All of them?

Paphlagonian
Are you surprised?
By god, I've got a chest jammed full of them.

Sausage Seller
I've got an attic and two apartments full.

Demos
Come on, let's have a look. These oracles—
who do they come from?

Paphlagonian
Mine are from Bacis.

Demos *[to the Sausage Seller]*
Who do yours come from?

Sausage Seller
They're from Glanis,
Bacis' elder brother.

Demos *[to the Paphlagonian]*
What are they about?

Paphlagonian
About Athens, about Pylos, about you,
about me, about everything.

Demos *[to the Sausage Seller]*
And yours?
What are they about?

ΑΛΛΑΝΤΟΠΩΛΗΣ

περὶ Ἀθηνῶν, περὶ φακῆς,
περὶ Λακεδαιμονίων, περὶ σκόμβρων νέων,
περὶ τῶν μετρούντων τἄλφιτ᾽ ἐν ἀγορᾷ κακῶς,
περὶ σοῦ, περὶ ἐμοῦ, περὶ ἁπάντων πραγμάτων.

ΔΗΜΟΣ

ἄγε νυν ὅπως αὐτοὺς ἀναγνώσεσθέ μοι,
καὶ τὸν περὶ ἐμοῦ 'κεῖνον ᾧπερ ἥδομαι,
ὡς ἐν νεφέλαισιν αἰετὸς γενήσομαι.

ΠΑΦΛΑΓΩΝΝ

ἄκουε δή νυν καὶ πρόσεχε τὸν νοῦν ἐμοί.
φράζευ Ἐρεχθεΐδη λογίων ὁδόν, ἥν σοι Ἀπόλλων
ἴαχεν ἐξ ἀδύτοιο διὰ τριπόδων ἐριτίμων.
σῴζεσθαί σ᾽ ἐκέλευσ᾽ ἱερὸν κύνα καρχαρόδοντα,
ὃς πρὸ σέθεν λάσκων καὶ ὑπὲρ σοῦ δεινὰ κεκραγὼς
σοὶ μισθὸνποριεῖ, κἂν μὴ δρᾷ ταῦτ᾽ ἀπολεῖται.
πολλοὶ γὰρ μίσει σφε κατακρώζουσι κολοιοί.

ΔΗΜΟΣ

ταυτὶ μὰ τὴν Δήμητρ᾽ ἐγὼ οὐκ οἶδ᾽ ὅ τι λέγει.
τί γάρ ἐστ᾽ Ἐρεχθεῖ καὶ κολοιοῖς καὶ κυνί;

ΠΑΦΛΑΓΩΝΝ

ἐγὼ μέν εἰμ᾽ ὁ κύων· πρὸ σοῦ γὰρ ἀπύω·
σοὶ δ᾽ εἶπε σῴζεσθαί μ᾽ ὁ Φοῖβος τὸν κύνα.

ΑΛΛΑΝΤΟΠΩΛΗΣ

οὐ τοῦτό φησ᾽ ὁ χρησμός, ἀλλ᾽ ὁ κύων ὁδὶ

SAUSAGE SELLER

They're about Athens,
about lentil soup, about the Spartans,
about fresh mackerel, about flour merchants
who give false measure in the marketplace,
about you, about me. That man there—

[He indicates the Paphlagonian.]

let him suck his own cock.

DEMOS

Well, come on then,
read them to me—especially that one
which I enjoy so much, that I'll become
an eagle in the clouds.[113]

PAPHLAGONIAN

Then listen,
and give me now your complete attention:

[The Paphlagonian reads from one of the scrolls.]

"Son of Erechtheus, hearken to the intent
of Apollo's oracles, which he pronounces
through holy tripods from his inner shrine.
He has ordered you to keep safe the sacred hound
with the jagged teeth who barks in your defence
and on your behalf yowls out alarming noises.
He will furnish you with payments, and if he fails,
he will go under, for there are countless jackdaws
who hate that dog and keep screaming after him."

DEMOS

By Demeter, I do not understand
a word he says. What does Erechtheus
have to do with jackdaws and a dog?

PAPHLAGONIAN

I am that dog. I howl in your defence.
Phoebus tells you to protect your dog—me.[114]

SAUSAGE SELLER

The oracle says nothing of the sort.
This dog here . . .

ὥσπερ θύρας σοῦ τῶν λογίων παρεσθίει.
ἐμοὶ γάρ ἐστ᾽ ὀρθῶς περὶ τούτου τοῦ κυνός.

ΔΗΜΟΣ

λέγε νυν· ἐγὼ δὲ πρῶτα λήψομαι λίθον,
ἵνα μή μ᾽ ὁ χρησμὸς τὸ πέος οὑτοσὶ δάκῃ.

ΑΛΛΑΝΤΟΠΩΛΗΣ

φράζευ Ἐρεχθεΐδη κύνα Κέρβερον ἀνδραποδιστήν,
ὃς κέρκῳ σαίνων σ᾽ ὁπόταν δειπνῇς ἐπιτηρῶν
ἐξέδεταί σου τοὔψον, ὅταν σύ ποι ἄλλοσε χάσκῃς·
ἐσφοιτῶν τ᾽ ἐς τοὐπτάνιον λήσει σε κυνηδὸν
νύκτωρ τὰς λοπάδας καὶ τὰς νήσους διαλείχων.

ΔΗΜΟΣ

νὴ τὸν Ποσειδῶ πολύ γ᾽ ἄμεινον ὦ Γλάνι.

ΠΑΦΛΑΓΩΝΝ

ὦ τᾶν ἄκουσον, εἶτα διάκρινον τόδε.
ἔστι γυνή, τέξει δὲ λέονθ᾽ ἱεραῖς ἐν Ἀθήναις,
ὃς περὶ τοῦ δήμου πολλοῖς κώνωψι μαχεῖται
ὥστε περὶ σκύμνοισι βεβηκώς· τὸν σὺ φυλάξαι,
τεῖχος ποιήσας ξύλινον πύργους τε σιδηροῦς.
ταῦτ᾽ οἶσθ᾽ ὅ τι λέγει;

ΔΗΜΟΣ

μὰ τὸν Ἀπόλλω ᾽γὼ μὲν οὔ.

ΠΑΦΛΑΓΩΝΝ

ἔφραζεν ὁ θεός σοι σαφῶς σῴζειν ἐμέ·
ἐγὼ γὰρ ἀντὶ τοῦ λέοντός εἰμί σοι.

ΔΗΜΟΣ

καὶ πῶς μ᾽ ἐλελήθης Ἀντιλέων γεγενημένος;

[The Sausage Seller points to the Paphlagonian.]

. . . is chewing up your oracles
the way dogs chew on doorposts. I have here
the proper prophecy about the dog.

DEMOS

Then state it. But first I'll pick up this stone,
so the oracle about the dog won't bite.

SAUSAGE SELLER *[pretending to read from his scroll]*

"Son of Erechtheus, beware of Cerberus,
the dog which kidnaps men.[115] When you are at a meal
he fawns on you with wagging tail, but he's watching
to devour your dishes, when you look away,
your mouth agape. Often in the night he sneaks
into your kitchen rooms, while you are unaware,
and, like a dog, licks clean your plates and islands."

DEMOS

By Poseidon, Glanis, that's much better!

PAPHLAGONIAN

Well, listen to this one and then decide:

[The Paphlagonian reads from another scroll.]

"A woman in sacred Athens will bear a lion,
who will fight for the people against huge clouds
of gnats, as if he were protecting his own cubs.
Look after him. Build wooden walls around him
and towers of iron."
Do you know what that means?

DEMOS

By Apollo, I don't.

PAPHLAGONIAN

The god clearly states
you should look after me, because I am
that lion symbol.

DEMOS

How did you become
the lion Simba without my knowledge?[116]

ΑΛΛΑΝΤΟΠΩΛΗΣ

ἓν οὐκ ἀναδιδάσκει σε τῶν λογίων ἑκών,
ὃ μόνον σιδηροῦν ἐστι τεῖχος καὶ ξύλον,
ἐν ᾧ σε σῴζειν τόνδ᾽ ἐκέλευσ᾽ ὁ Λοξίας.

ΔΗΜΟΣ

πῶς δῆτα τοῦτ᾽ ἔφραζεν ὁ θεός;

ΑΛΛΑΝΤΟΠΩΛΗΣ

τουτονὶ
δῆσαί σ᾽ ἐκέλευ᾽ ἐν πεντεσυρίγγῳ ξύλῳ.

ΔΗΜΟΣ

ταυτὶ τελεῖσθαι τὰ λόγι᾽ ἤδη μοι δοκεῖ.

ΠΑΦΛΑΓΩΝΝ

μὴ πείθου· φθονεραὶ γὰρ ἐπικρώζουσι κορῶναι.
ἀλλ᾽ ἱέρακα φίλει μεμνημένος ἐν φρεσὶν ὅς σοι
ἤγαγε συνδήσας Λακεδαιμονίων κορακίνους.

ΑΛΛΑΝΤΟΠΩΛΗΣ

τοῦτό γέ τοι Παφλαγὼν παρεκινδύνευσε μεθυσθείς.
Κεκροπίδη κακόβουλε τί τοῦθ᾽ ἡγεῖ μέγα τοὔργον;
καί κε γυνὴ φέροι ἄχθος, ἐπεί κεν ἀνὴρ ἀναθείη·
ἀλλ᾽ οὐκ ἂν μαχέσαιτο· χέσαιτο γάρ, εἰ μαχέσαιτο.

ΠΑΦΛΑΓΩΝΝ

ἀλλὰ τόδε φράσσαι, πρὸ Πύλου Πύλον ἥν σοι ἔφραζεν.
ἔστι Πύλος πρὸ Πύλοιο—

SAUSAGE SELLER

He's quite deliberately not explaining
something in that saying—the only wall
made out of iron and wood inside which
Loxias has told you to preserve the man.[117]

DEMOS

Why does the god say these words?

SAUSAGE SELLER

He's telling you
to tie this man down in those wooden stocks,
the ones which have five holes.[118]

DEMOS

I think that oracle
is just about to be fulfilled.

PAPHLAGONIAN

Don't believe him!
The crows are jealous. They keep cawing at me.

[The Paphlagonian reads from another scroll.]

"Cherish the hawk, and remember in your heart
he was the one who on your behalf brought back
those young Spartan ravens all chained together."

SAUSAGE SELLER

The Paphlagonian was drunk that day—
that's why he took such a dangerous risk.

[The Sausage Seller pretends to read from one of his scrolls.]

"O poorly counselled son of Cecrops, why believe
that was a mighty deed?[119] For even a woman
can bear a load if a man places it on her.
But she won't fight."

[The Sausage Seller points to the Paphlagonian.]

If he went into battle,
he'd crap his pants.

PAPHLAGONIAN

But consider the phrase
"Pylos before Pylos," something the god
has drawn to your attention—there is
"A Pylos before Pylos."

ΔΗΜΟΣ

τί τοῦτο λέγει, πρὸ Πύλοιο;

ΑΛΛΑΝΤΟΠΩΛΗΣ

τὰς πυέλους φησὶν καταλήψεσθ' ἐν βαλανείῳ.

ΔΗΜΟΣ

ἐγὼ δ' ἄλουτος τήμερον γενήσομαι;

ΑΛΛΑΝΤΟΠΩΛΗΣ

οὗτος γὰρ ἡμῶν τὰς πυέλους ἀφήρπασεν.
ἀλλ' οὑτοσὶ γάρ ἐστι περὶ τοῦ ναυτικοῦ
ὁ χρησμός, ᾧ σε δεῖ προσέχειν τὸν νοῦν πάνυ.

ΔΗΜΟΣ

προσέχω· σὺ δ' ἀναγίγνωσκε, τοῖς ναύταισί μου
ὅπως ὁ μισθὸς πρῶτον ἀποδοθήσεται.

ΑΛΛΑΝΤΟΠΩΛΗΣ

Αἰγεΐδη φράσσαι κυναλώπεκα, μή σε δολώσῃ,
λαίθαργον ταχύπουν, δολίαν κερδὼ πολύιδριν.
οἶσθ' ὅ τι ἐστὶν τοῦτο;

ΔΗΜΟΣ

Φιλόστρατος ἡ κυναλώπηξ.

ΑΛΛΑΝΤΟΠΩΛΗΣ

οὐ τοῦτό φησιν, ἀλλὰ ναῦς ἑκάστοτε
αἰτεῖ ταχείας ἀργυρολόγους οὑτοσί·
ταύτας ἀπαυδᾷ μὴ διδόναι σ' ὁ Λοξίας.

ΔΗΜΟΣ

πῶς δὴ τριήρης ἐστὶ κυναλώπηξ;

ΑΛΛΑΝΤΟΠΩΛΗΣ

ὅπως;
ὅτι ἡ τριήρης ἐστὶ χὠ κύων ταχύ.

DEMOS

What does he mean
by that expression "Pylos before Pylos"?[120]

SAUSAGE SELLER

He's saying he will pile up piles of bath tubs
and take them from the wash house.[121]

DEMOS

So today
I won't be having my bath?

SAUSAGE SELLER

No, you won't,
since he's taken away our tubs. Here's one—
an oracle about the fleet. You should
give it your very close attention.

DEMOS

I'm listening. You read it. First of all,
how my sailors are going to get their pay.

SAUSAGE SELLER *[pretending to read from a scroll]*

"Son of Aegeus, beware of the fox-dog,
in case he tricks you. He's full of deceit,
runs fast, and is cunning and resourceful."
Do you know what that means?

DEMOS

Well, the dog fox—
that's Philostratus.[122]

SAUSAGE SELLER

That's not what it says.
It's about the fast ships which collect the cash,
the ones this fellow here keeps requesting.[123]
Loxias is telling you not to give them.

DEMOS

How does a warship become a fox dog?

SAUSAGE SELLER

How come? Because warships and fox dogs
both move fast.

ΔΗΜΟΣ

πῶς οὖν ἀλώπηξ προσετέθη πρὸς τῷ κυνί;

ΑΛΛΑΝΤΟΠΩΛΗΣ

ἀλωπεκίοισι τοὺς στρατιώτας ᾔκασεν,
ὁτιὴ βότρυς τρώγουσιν ἐν τοῖς χωρίοις.

ΔΗΜΟΣ

εἶεν·
τούτοις ὁ μισθὸς τοῖς ἀλωπεκίοισι ποῦ;

ΑΛΛΑΝΤΟΠΩΛΗΣ

ἐγὼποριῶ, καὶ τοῦτον ἡμερῶν τριῶν.
ἀλλ᾽ ἔτι τόνδ᾽ ἐπάκουσον, ὃν εἶπέ σοι ἐξαλέασθαι
χρησμὸν Λητοΐδης, Κυλλήνην, μή σε δολώσῃ.

ΔΗΜΟΣ

ποίαν Κυλλήνην;

ΑΛΛΑΝΤΟΠΩΛΗΣ

τὴν τούτου χεῖρ᾽ ἐποίησεν
Κυλλήνην ὀρθῶς, ὁτιή φησ᾽, 'ἔμβαλε κυλλῇ.'

ΠΑΦΛΑΓΩΝΝ

οὐκ ὀρθῶς φράζει· τὴν Κυλλήνην γὰρ ὁ Φοῖβος
ἐς τὴν χεῖρ᾽ ὀρθῶς ᾐνίξατο τὴν Διοπείθους.
ἀλλὰ γάρ ἐστιν ἐμοὶ χρησμὸς περὶ σοῦ πτερυγωτός,
αἰετὸς ὡς γίγνει καὶ πάσης γῆς βασιλεύεις.

ΑΛΛΑΝΤΟΠΩΛΗΣ

καὶ γὰρ ἐμοί· καὶ γῆς καὶ τῆς ἐρυθρᾶς γε θαλάσσης,
χὤτι γ᾽ ἐν Ἐκβατάνοις δικάσεις, λείχων ἐπίπαστα.

DEMOS

Then why does it say fox dog
instead of just a dog?

SAUSAGE SELLER

It's a comparison.
It's saying fox dogs resemble soldiers,
who, like them, feed on grapes from vineyards.[124]

DEMOS

All right, then. Where's the pay for these fox cubs?

SAUSAGE SELLER

I'll see to that and within three days, too.
But pay attention to this oracle,
where Leto's son tells you to shun the port
called Crooked Harbour—that place may trick you.[125]

DEMOS

What's Crooked Harbour?

SAUSAGE SELLER *[indicating the Paphlagonian]*

It clearly states here
that Crooked Harbour is this fellow's hand—
since he's always saying, "My hand's crooked,
so put something in it."

PAPHLAGONIAN

He's telling lies!
The correct reading of that cryptic saying
is that Phoebus means by "Crooked Harbour"
the hand of Diopeithes.[126] But look here,
I have an oracle with wings—about you.
You will become an eagle and a king
ruling all the earth.

SAUSAGE SELLER

I have one, as well—
you will rule the Earth and the Red Sea, too,
be a presiding judge in Ebatana
and lick up decorated cakes.[127]

ΠΑΦΛΑΓΩΝΝ

ἀλλ᾽ ἐγὼ εἶδον ὄναρ, καί μοὐδόκει ἡ θεὸς αὐτὴ
τοῦ δήμου καταχεῖν ἀρυταίνῃ πλουθυγίειαν.

ΑΛΛΑΝΤΟΠΩΛΗΣ

νὴ Δία καὶ γὰρ ἐγώ· καί μοὐδόκει ἡ θεὸς αὐτὴ
ἐκ πόλεως ἐλθεῖν καὶ γλαῦξ αὐτῇ ‘πικαθῆσθαι·
εἶτα καταspένδειν κατὰ τῆς κεφαλῆς ἀρυβάλλῳ
ἀμβροσίαν κατὰ σοῦ, κατὰ τούτου δὲ σκοροδάλμην.

ΔΗΜΟΣ

ἰοὺ ἰού.
οὐκ ἦν ἄρ᾽ οὐδεὶς τοῦ Γλάνιδος σοφώτερος.
καὶ νῦν ἐμαυτὸν ἐπιτρέπω σοι τουτονὶ
γεροντagωγεῖν κἀναπαιδεύειν πάλιν.

ΠΑΦΛΑΓΩΝΝ

μήπω γ᾽, ἱκετεύω σ᾽, ἀλλ᾽ ἀνάμεινον, ὡς ἐγὼ
κριθὰςποριῶ σοι καὶ βίον καθ᾽ ἡμέραν.

ΔΗΜΟΣ

οὐκ ἀνέχομαι κριθῶν ἀκούων· πολλάκις
ἐξηπατήθην ὑπό τε σοῦ καὶ Θουφάνους.

ΠΑΦΛΑΓΩΝΝ

ἀλλ᾽ ἄλφιτ᾽ ἤδη σοι ποριῶ ’σκευασμένα.

ΑΛΛΑΝΤΟΠΩΛΗΣ

ἐγὼ δὲ μαζίσκας γε διαμεμαγμένας
καὶ τοὔψον ὀπτόν· μηδὲν ἄλλ᾽ εἰ μὴ ’σθιε.

PAPHLAGONIAN

In a dream
I have seen Athena herself. I saw her
pouring health and wealth all over Demos
with a bucket.

SAUSAGE SELLER

I've seen the goddess, too.
I saw her come in person, moving out
from the Acropolis—she had an owl
perched on her helmet. Then over your head
she poured ambrosia from a little jug,
and over his head . . .

[He indicates the Paphlagonian]

. . . she dumped pickled garlic.

DEMOS

That's splendid! It's really true that no one
is cleverer than Glanis. And so now
I commit myself to you, to guide me
in my old age and to educate me
once more from the start.

PAPHLAGONIAN

No, no! Not yet!
I'm begging you. Just wait a little while,
so I can provide some barley for you
and what you need to live on every day.

DEMOS

I can't stand to hear you talk of barley.
I've been cheated too many times by you
and by Thuphanes.[128]

PAPHLAGONIAN

How about flour cakes?
I'll provide some, especially for you!

SAUSAGE SELLER

I'll give you
well-kneaded scones and nicely roasted meat,
All you have to do is eat it.

ΔΗΜΟΣ

ἀνύσατέ νυν ὅ τι περ ποιήσεθ᾽· ὡς ἐγώ,
ὁπότερος ἂν σφῷν νῦν με μᾶλλον εὖ ποιῇ,
τούτῳ παραδώσω τῆς πυκνὸς τὰς ἡνίας.

ΠΑΦΛΑΓΩΝΝ

τρέχοιμ᾽ ἂν εἴσω πρότερος.

ΑΛΛΑΝΤΟΠΩΛΗΣ

οὐ δῆτ᾽ ἀλλ᾽ ἐγώ.

ΧΟΡΟΣ

ὦ Δῆμε καλήν γ᾽ ἔχεις
ἀρχήν, ὅτε πάντες ἄνθρωποι
δεδίασί σ᾽ ὥσπερ
ἄνδρα τύραννον.
ἀλλ᾽ εὐπαράγωγος εἶ,
θωπευόμενός τε χαίρεις
κἀξαπατώμενος,
πρὸς τόν τε λέγοντ᾽ ἀεὶ
κέχηνας· ὁ νοῦς δέ σου
παρὼν ἀποδημεῖ.

ΔΗΜΟΣ

νοῦς οὐκ ἔνι ταῖς κόμαις
ὑμῶν, ὅτε μ᾽ οὐ φρονεῖν
νομίζετ᾽· ἐγὼ δ᾽ ἑκὼν
ταῦτ᾽ ἠλιθιάζω.
αὐτός τε γὰρ ἥδομαι
βρύλλων τὸ καθ᾽ ἡμέραν,
κλέπτοντά τε βούλομαι
τρέφειν ἕνα προστάτην·
τοῦτον δ᾽, ὅταν ᾖ πλέως,
ἄρας ἐπάταξα.

DEMOS

All right.
Get a move on with what you're going to do.
Then I'll hand over the keys to the Pnyx
to whichever one of you is better
at giving me good service.

PAPHLAGONIAN

I'll be the first
to run inside.

SAUSAGE SELLER

No you won't. I will!

[The Paphlagonian and the Sausage Seller both rush into the house.]

CHORUS

O Demos your rule
is surely so fine,
you're like a tyrant
men fear all the time.
But you're easy to fool—
you like flattering cries
and love to be praised
and told plenty of lies.
You listen to speakers
with mouth open wide
your mind may be present
but it's gone for a ride.

DEMOS

If you think I'm a dolt,
then beneath your long hair
you've got no brain at all.
I am fully aware
that I act like a fool—
I like drinking each day,
and I raise up a thief
for political sway,
with this purpose in mind—
when he's stuffed himself fat,
then I lift up my hand
and knock him down flat.

ΧΟΡΟΣ

χοὔτω μὲν ἂν εὖ ποιοῖς,
εἴ σοι πυκνότης ἔνεστ᾽
ἐν τῷ τρόπῳ, ὡς λέγεις,
  τούτῳ πάνυ πολλή,
εἰ τούσδ᾽ ἐπίτηδες ὥσπερ
δημοσίους τρέφεις
ἐν τῇ πυκνί, κᾆθ᾽ ὅταν
μή σοι τύχῃ ὄψον ὄν,
τούτων ὃς ἂν ᾖ παχύς,
  θύσας ἐπιδειπνεῖς.

ΔΗΜΟΣ

σκέψασθε δέ μ᾽, εἰ σοφῶς
αὑτοὺς περιέρχομαι
τοὺς οἰομένους φρονεῖν
  κἄμ᾽ ἐξαπατύλλειν.
τηρῶ γὰρ ἑκάστοτ᾽ αὐτοὺς
οὐδὲ δοκῶν ὁρᾶν
κλέπτοντας· ἔπειτ᾽ ἀναγκάζω
πάλιν ἐξεμεῖν
ἅττ᾽ ἂν κεκλόφωσί μου,
  κημὸν καταμηλῶν.

ΠΑΦΛΑΓΩΝΝ

ἄπαγ᾽ ἐς μακαρίαν ἐκποδών.

ΑΛΛΑΝΤΟΠΩΛΗΣ

σύ γ᾽ ὦ φθόρε.

ΠΑΦΛΑΓΩΝΝ

ὦ Δῆμ᾽ ἐγὼ μέντοι παρεσκευασμένος
τρίπαλαι κάθημαι βουλόμενός σ᾽ εὐεργετεῖν.

ΑΛΛΑΝΤΟΠΩΛΗΣ

ἐγὼ δὲ δεκάπαλαί γε καὶ δωδεκάπαλαι
καὶ χιλιόπαλαι καὶ προπαλαιπαλαίπαλαι.

CHORUS

What you do then is good,
and your style, as you say,
in these things is profound,
if you use a sly way
to keep raising these men
like our victims of state.
They grow great on the Pnyx,
so you won't have to wait.
Then you take one who's fat,
if you need to eat meat,
set him up as an offering
and have something to eat.[129]

DEMOS

Look at me—I am smart.
I deceive all those men
who think they're so clever
and can fool me again.
I'm on watch for them all,
and my eye always looks
though I don't seem to see,
when they're acting like crooks.
Then I make them throw up
what they've stolen from folk—
on the voting urn top
they all puke when I poke.[130]

[The Paphlagonian and the Sausage Seller return from the house. They are each carrying a chest full of food and are getting in each other's way.]

PAPHLAGONIAN

Get the devil out of my way!

SAUSAGE SELLER

Shove off!

PAPHLAGONIAN

Demos, for a long, long time I've been here
sitting ready, really keen to serve you.

SAUSAGE SELLER

And I've been ready for ages and ages—
ten, twelve, a thousand—an infinite time.

ΔΗΜΟΣ

ἐγὼ δὲ προσδοκῶν γε τρισμυριόπαλαι
βδελύττομαί σφω καὶ προπαλαιπαλαίπαλαι.

ΑΛΛΑΝΤΟΠΩΛΗΣ

οἶσθ' οὖν ὃ δρᾶσον;

ΔΗΜΟΣ

εἰ δὲ μή, φράσεις γε σύ.

ΑΛΛΑΝΤΟΠΩΛΗΣ

ἄφες ἀπὸ βαλβίδων ἐμέ τε καὶ τουτονί,
ἵνα σ' εὖ ποιῶμεν ἐξ ἴσου.

ΔΗΜΟΣ

δρᾶν ταῦτα χρή.
ἄπιτον.

ΠΑΦΛΑΓΩΝ καὶ ΑΛΛΑΝΤΟΠΩΛΗΣ

ἰδού.

ΔΗΜΟΣ

θέοιτ' ἄν.

ΑΛΛΑΝΤΟΠΩΛΗΣ

ὑποθεῖν οὐκ ἐῶ.

ΔΗΜΟΣ

ἀλλ' ἦ μεγάλως εὐδαιμονήσω τήμερον
ὑπὸ τῶν ἐραστῶν νὴ Δί' ἢ 'γὼ θρύψομαι.

ΠΑΦΛΑΓΩΝΝ

ὁρᾷς; ἐγώ σοι πρότερος ἐκφέρω δίφρον.

ΑΛΛΑΝΤΟΠΩΛΗΣ

ἀλλ' οὐ τράπεζαν, ἀλλ' ἐγὼ προτεραίτερος.

DEMOS

I've been waiting thirty thousand ages,
fed up with you both for an eternity.

SAUSAGE SELLER

You know what you should do?

DEMOS

I will if you tell me.

SAUSAGE SELLER

Send me and him out from a starting line,
so we can race to see who serves you best—
under the same conditions.

DEMOS

That we must do.
Get in line.[131]

[The Paphlagonian and the Sausage Seller assume the positions of sprinters about to race off.]

PAPHLAGONIAN AND SAUSAGE SELLER

Ready!

DEMOS

Then off you go!

[The Paphlagonian and the Sausage Seller race off to their separate chests and piles of stuff.]

SAUSAGE SELLER

I won't let you win by some secret trick!

DEMOS

By god, today my lovers will make me
extremely happy or else I'll have to
keep playing the coy coquette.

PAPHLAGONIAN *[running back to Demos]*

Look at this!
I'm the first here—I'm bringing you a chair!

SAUSAGE SELLER

But not a table—I was the first with that.

ΠΑΦΛΑΓΩΝΝ

ἰδοὺ φέρω σοι τήνδε μαζίσκην ἐγὼ
ἐκ τῶν ὀλῶν τῶν ἐκ Πύλου μεμαγμένην.

ΑΛΛΑΝΤΟΠΩΛΗΣ

ἐγὼ δὲ μυστίλας μεμυστιλημένας
ὑπὸ τῆς θεοῦ τῇ χειρὶ τἠλεφαντίνῃ.

ΔΗΜΟΣ

ὡς μέγαν ἄρ᾽ εἶχες ὦ πότνια τὸν δάκτυλον.

ΠΑΦΛΑΓΩΝΝ

ἐγὼ δ᾽ ἔτνος γε πίσινον εὔχρων καὶ καλόν·
ἐτόρυνε δ᾽ αὔθ᾽ ἡ Παλλὰς ἡ Πυλαιμάχος.

ΑΛΛΑΝΤΟΠΩΛΗΣ

ὦ Δῆμ᾽ ἐναργῶς ἡ θεός σ᾽ ἐπισκοπεῖ,
καὶ νῦν ὑπερέχει σου χύτραν ζωμοῦ πλέαν.

ΔΗΜΟΣ

οἴει γὰρ οἰκεῖσθ᾽ ἂν ἔτι τήνδε τὴν πόλιν,
εἰ μὴ φανερῶς ἡμῶν ὑπερεῖχε τὴν χύτραν;

ΠΑΦΛΑΓΩΝΝ

τουτὶ τέμαχός σοὔδωκεν ἡ Φοβεσιστράτη.

ΑΛΛΑΝΤΟΠΩΛΗΣ

ἡ δ᾽ Ὀβριμοπάτρα γ᾽ ἑφθὸν ἐκ ζωμοῦ κρέας
καὶ χόλικος ἠνύστρου τε καὶ γαστρὸς τόμον.

ΔΗΜΟΣ

καλῶς γ᾽ ἐποίησε τοῦ πέπλου μεμνημένη.

ΠΑΦΛΑΓΩΝΝ

ἡ Γοργολόφα σ᾽ ἐκέλευε τουτοὺ φαγεῖν
ἐλατῆρος, ἵνα τὰς ναῦς ἐλαύνωμεν καλῶς.

Paphlagonian

Look at this. I've brought you barley cake
prepared by hand with grain from Pylos.

Sausage Seller

I've got some scooped out bread crusts. They were made
by the goddess' ivory hand.

Demos

Lady Athena,
how huge your fingers are![132]

Paplagonian

I have pea soup—
tasty and a splendid colour. Pallas,
who fought at Pylos, stirred it herself.

Sausage Seller

O Demos, the goddess is watching you—
that's clear enough—and now above your head
she holds a pot brim full of broth.

Demos

Do you think
we'd still be inhabiting this city
if she was not clearly holding over us
a pan of broth?

Paphlagonian

And here's a slice of fish—
it's a present to you from the goddess
who strikes panic into every army.

Sausage Seller

And here is meat cooked in its own juices
from the daughter of a mighty father—
along with a slice of tripe and sausage.

Demos

She's remembering the robe I gave her.
That's nice.

Paphlagonian

The goddess of the dreadful plume
bids you eat this pound cake—our ships oarsmen
will row faster with these currants.[133]

ΑΛΛΑΝΤΟΠΩΛΗΣ
λαβὲ καὶ ταδί νυν.

ΔΗΜΟΣ
καὶ τί τούτοις χρήσομαι
τοῖς ἐντέροις;

ΑΛΛΑΝΤΟΠΩΛΗΣ
ἐπίτηδες αὔτ᾽ ἔπεμψέ σοι
ἐς τὰς τριήρεις ἐντερόνειαν ἡ θεός·
ἐπισκοπεῖ γὰρ περιφανῶς τὸ ναυτικόν.
ἔχε καὶ πιεῖν κεκραμένον τρία καὶ δύο.

ΔΗΜΟΣ
ὡς ἡδὺς ὦ Ζεῦ καὶ τὰ τρία φέρων καλῶς.

ΑΛΛΑΝΤΟΠΩΛΗΣ
ἡ Τριτογενὴς γὰρ αὐτὸν ἐνετριτώνισεν.

ΠΑΦΛΑΓΩΝΝ
λαβέ νυν πλακοῦντος πίονος παρ᾽ ἐμοῦ τόμον.

ΑΛΛΑΝΤΟΠΩΛΗΣ
παρ᾽ ἐμοῦ δ᾽ ὅλον γε τὸν πλακοῦντα τουτονί.

ΠΑΦΛΑΓΩΝΝ
ἀλλ᾽ οὐ λαγῷ᾽ ἕξεις ὁπόθεν δῷς, ἀλλ᾽ ἐγώ.

ΑΛΛΑΝΤΟΠΩΛΗΣ
οἴμοι, πόθεν λαγῷά μοι γενήσεται;
ὦ θυμὲ νυνὶ βωμολόχον ἔξευρέ τι.

ΠΑΦΛΑΓΩΝΝ
ὁρᾷς τάδ᾽ ὦ κακόδαιμον;

ΑΛΛΑΝΤΟΠΩΛΗΣ
ὀλίγον μοι μέλει·
ἐκεινοὶ γὰρ ὡς ἔμ᾽ ἔρχονταί τινες
πρέσβεις ἔχοντες ἀργυρίου βαλλάντια.

SAUSAGE SELLER

Take this, too.

DEMOS

What do I do with these bits of stomach?

SAUSAGE SELLER

The goddess sends these to you on purpose—
to fix our ships bellies. That makes it clear
her eye is on our fleet. Have a drink now,
two measures of wine and one of water.[134]

DEMOS *[sampling the wine]*

Ah Zeus, how delicious that is—that mix
of wine and water blends so perfectly.

SAUSAGE SELLER

Athena, thrice born, mixed all three parts.[135]

PAPHLAGONIAN

Here, take this slice of rich flat-cake from me.

SAUSAGE SELLER

But from me you will get an entire cake.

PAPHLAGONIAN

But you don't have stewed hare to give him. I do!

SAUSAGE SELLER *[to himself]*

Damn and blast it! Where can I get a hare?
Come on, brain, produce some devious trick.[136]

PAPHLAGONIAN *[pulling a hare from his supply]*

You see this, you miserable devil!

SAUSAGE SELLER *[looking into the wings]*

I don't give a damn. I see men coming—
ambassadors bringing bags of cash to me.

PAPHLAGONIAN *[putting the hare down and moving toward the wings]*

Where? Where are they?

SAUSAGE SELLER *[grabbing the hare]*

What do you care?
Can't you ever stop bothering foreigners?
My dear little Demos, you see this hare—
I'm bringing it for you.

ΠΑΦΛΑΓΩΝΝ

ποῦ ποῦ;

ΑΛΛΑΝΤΟΠΩΛΗΣ

τί δέ σοι τοῦτ'; οὐκ ἐάσεις τοὺς ξένους;
ὦ Δημίδιον ὁρᾷς τὰ λαγῴ' ἅ σοι φέρω;

ΠΑΦΛΑΓΩΝΝ

οἴμοι τάλας ἀδίκως γε τἄμ' ὑφήρπασας.

ΑΛΛΑΝΤΟΠΩΛΗΣ

νὴ τὸν Ποσειδῶ καὶ σὺ γὰρ τοὺς ἐκ Πύλου.

ΔΗΜΟΣ

εἴπ', ἀντιβολῶ, πῶς ἐπενόησας ἁρπάσαι;

ΑΛΛΑΝΤΟΠΩΛΗΣ

τὸ μὲν νόημα τῆς θεοῦ, τὸ δὲ κλέμμ' ἐμόν.

ΠΑΦΛΑΓΩΝΝ

ἐγὼ δ' ἐκινδύνευσ', ἐγὼ δ' ὤπτησά γε.

ΔΗΜΟΣ

ἄπιθ'· οὐ γὰρ ἀλλὰ τοῦ παραθέντος ἡ χάρις.

ΠΑΦΛΑΓΩΝΝ

οἴμοι κακοδαίμων, ὑπεραναιδευθήσομαι.

ΑΛΛΑΝΤΟΠΩΛΗΣ

τί οὐ διακρίνεις Δῆμ' ὁπότερός ἐστι νῷν
ἀνὴρ ἀμείνων περὶ σὲ καὶ τὴν γαστέρα;

ΔΗΜΟΣ

τῷ δῆτ' ἂν ὑμᾶς χρησάμενος τεκμηρίῳ
δόξαιμι κρίνειν τοῖς θεαταῖσιν σοφῶς;

ΑΛΛΑΝΤΟΠΩΛΗΣ

ἐγὼ φράσω σοι. τὴν ἐμὴν κίστην ἰὼν
ξύλλαβε σιωπῇ καὶ βασάνισον ἅττ' ἔνι,
καὶ τὴν Παφλαγόνος· κἀμέλει κρινεῖς καλῶς.

PAPHLAGONIAN

You bloody cheat!
You've stolen my stuff! That's not fair!

SAUSAGE SELLER

Yes, I have,
by Poseidon, just as you nicked those men
from Pylos.

DEMOS *[to the Sausage Seller]*

If you don't mind my asking,
tell me this—how did you get that idea
to steal the hare?

SAUSAGE SELLER

The idea is from Athena,
but the theft is all my own.

PAPHLAGONIAN

I took the risk,
and, in addition, I prepared the meat.

DEMOS

Get out of here. The one who brings the food
is the only one to get my grateful thanks.

PAPHLAGONIAN *[aside]*

Good god, his shamelessness will conquer mine!

SAUSAGE SELLER

All right, Demos, why not judge which of us
was the best to you and to your stomach?

DEMOS

How do I decide between the two of you,
using facts that will make the audience
believe the judgment I pronounce is wise?

SAUSAGE SELLER *[pulling Demos aside and lowering his voice]*

I'll tell you. Don't say a word. Go over there
to my basket. Check out what's inside it.
Then, do that to the Paphlagonian's.
That's all you need to judge correctly.

ΔΗΜΟΣ

φέρ' ἴδω τί οὖν ἔνεστιν;

ΑΛΛΑΝΤΟΠΩΛΗΣ

οὐχ ὁρᾷς κενὴν
ὦ παππίδιον; ἅπαντα γάρ σοι παρεφόρουν.

ΔΗΜΟΣ

αὕτη μὲν ἡ κίστη τὰ τοῦ Δήμου φρονεῖ.

ΑΛΛΑΝΤΟΠΩΛΗΣ

βάδιζέ νυν καὶ δεῦρο πρὸς τὴν Παφλαγόνος.
ὁρᾷς τάδ';

ΔΗΜΟΣ

οἴμοι τῶν ἀγαθῶν ὅσων πλέα.
ὅσον τὸ χρῆμα τοῦ πλακοῦντος ἀπέθετο·
ἐμοὶ δ' ἔδωκεν ἀποτεμὼν τυννουτονί.

ΑΛΛΑΝΤΟΠΩΛΗΣ

τοιαῦτα μέντοι καὶ πρότερόν σ' ἠργάζετο·
σοὶ μὲν προσεδίδου μικρὸν ὧν ἐλάμβανεν,
αὐτὸς δ' ἑαυτῷ παρετίθει τὰ μείζονα.

ΔΗΜΟΣ

ὦ μιαρὲ κλέπτων δή με ταῦτ' ἐξηπάτας;
ἐγὼ δέ τυ ἐστεφάνιξα κἀδωρησάμαν.

ΠΑΦΛΑΓΩΝΝ

ἐγὼ δ' ἔκλεπτον ἐπ' ἀγαθῷ γε τῇ πόλει.

ΔΗΜΟΣ

κατάθου ταχέως τὸν στέφανον, ἵν' ἐγὼ τουτῳὶ
αὐτὸν περιθῶ.

ΑΛΛΑΝΤΟΠΩΛΗΣ

κατάθου ταχέως μαστιγία.

DEMOS *[moving to the Sausage Seller's hamper]*
Well then, let's see. What's in here?

SAUSAGE SELLER
It's empty.
Can't you see that? My dear little father,
I brought everything to you.

DEMOS
This hamper
is on the people's side.

SAUSAGE SELLER
Now, stroll over here
to the Paphlagonian's. Do you see?

DEMOS
O my, it's full of so many good things!
A huge piece of cake he's keeping for himself!
He cut off a slice and gave that to me—
only this big!

SAUSAGE SELLER
That's what he did before.
He gave you a tiny part of what he took
and set aside most of it for himself.

DEMOS *[to the Paphlagonian]*
You wretch! Was that how you were cheating me,
by stealing? That symbol of your office—
I gave it to you.[137] I showered you with gifts.

PAPHLAGONIAN
I did steal, but for the city's benefit.

DEMOS
Take that badge off—and quickly, so that I
can give it to this man.

SAUSAGE SELLER
Hand it over fast.
You worthless rogue, you deserve a whipping.

ΠΑΦΛΑΓΩΝΝ

οὐ δῆτ᾽, ἐπεί μοι χρησμός ἐστι Πυθικὸς
φράζων ὑφ᾽ οὗ †δεήσει μ᾽† ἡττᾶσθαι μόνου.

ΑΛΛΑΝΤΟΠΩΛΗΣ

τοὐμόν γε φράζων ὄνομα καὶ λίαν σαφῶς.

ΠΑΦΛΑΓΩΝΝ

καὶ μήν σ᾽ ἐλέγξαι βούλομαι τεκμηρίῳ,
εἴ τι ξυνοίσεις τοῦ θεοῦ τοῖς θεσφάτοις.
καί σου τοσοῦτον πρῶτον ἐκπειράσομαι·
παῖς ὢν ἐφοίτας ἐς τίνος διδασκάλου;

ΑΛΛΑΝΤΟΠΩΛΗΣ

ἐν ταῖσιν εὔστραις κονδύλοις ἡρμοττόμην.

ΠΑΦΛΑΓΩΝΝ

πῶς εἶπας; ὥς μου χρησμὸς ἅπτεται φρενῶν.
εἶεν.
ἐν παιδοτρίβου δὲ τίνα πάλην ἐμάνθανες;

ΑΛΛΑΝΤΟΠΩΛΗΣ

κλέπτων ἐπιορκεῖν καὶ βλέπειν ἐναντίον·

ΠΑΦΛΑΓΩΝΝ

ὦ Φοῖβ᾽ Ἄπολλον Λύκιε τί ποτέ μ᾽ ἐργάσει;
τέχνην δὲ τίνα ποτ᾽ εἶχες ἐξανδρούμενος;

ΑΛΛΑΝΤΟΠΩΛΗΣ

ἠλλαντοπώλουν καί τι καὶ βινεσκόμην.

PAPHLAGONIAN

No. There is a Pythian oracle
which reveals the name of the only man
who destiny says will overthrow me.

SAUSAGE SELLER

It spoke my name, and it was very clear.

PAPHLAGONIAN

All right. I wish to put you through a test
with certain evidence, to make quite sure
you match what the god intended. And so
I will start by examining who you are.
As a boy, what schooling did you go through?

SAUSAGE SELLER

I was taught in the pits by being thrashed
where pigs are singed.

PAPHLAGONIAN

What's that you just said?

[Aside to himself]

That oracle will give me a heart attack!

[Returns to questioning the Sausage Seller]

All right. What did you learn from the teacher
in charge of wrestling?

SAUSAGE SELLER

Well, I learned this—
when I was stealing, I looked straight ahead
and told a lie.

PAPHLAGONIAN *[aside to himself]*

"O Phoebus Apollo,
lord of Lycia, what will you do to me?"[138]

[Resuming questioning the Sausage Seller]

When you were grown up, what was your trade?

SAUSAGE SELLER

I sold sausages and fucked a bit for cash.

ΠΑΦΛΑΓΩΝΝ

οἴμοι κακοδαίμων· οὐκέτ᾽ οὐδέν εἰμ᾽ ἐγώ.
λεπτή τις ἐλπίς ἐστ᾽ ἐφ᾽ ἧς ὀχούμεθα.
καί μοι τοσοῦτον εἰπέ· πότερον ἐν ἀγορᾷ
ἠλλαντοπώλεις ἐτεὸν ἢ ᾽πὶ ταῖς πύλαις;

ΑΛΛΑΝΤΟΠΩΛΗΣ

ἐπὶ ταῖς πύλαισιν, οὗ τὸ τάριχος ὤνιον.

ΠΑΦΛΑΓΩΝΝ

οἴμοι πέπρακται τοῦ θεοῦ τὸ θέσφατον.
κυλίνδετ᾽ εἴσω τόνδε τὸν δυσδαίμονα.
ὦ στέφανε χαίρων ἄπιθι, κεἴ σ᾽ ἄκων ἐγὼ
λείπω· σὲ δ᾽ ἄλλος τις λαβὼν κεκτήσεται,
κλέπτης μὲν οὐκ ἂν μᾶλλον, εὐτυχὴς δ᾽ ἴσως.

ΑΛΛΑΝΤΟΠΩΛΗΣ

Ἑλλάνιε Ζεῦ σὸν τὸ νικητήριον.

ΧΟΡΟΣ

ὦ χαῖρε καλλίνικε καὶ μέμνησ᾽ ὅτι
ἀνὴρ γεγένησαι δι᾽ ἐμέ· καί σ᾽ αἰτῶ βραχύ,
ὅπως ἔσομαί σοι Φανὸς ὑπογραφεὺς δικῶν.

ΔΗΜΟΣ

ἐμοὶ δέ γ᾽ ὅ τι σοι τοὔνομ᾽ εἴπ᾽.

ΑΛΛΑΝΤΟΠΩΛΗΣ

Ἀγοράκριτος·
ἐν τἀγορᾷ γὰρ κρινόμενος ἐβοσκόμην.

PAPHLAGONIAN *[aside to himself]*

My god, I'm screwed! I'm nothing anymore!
But I'm still riding on one slender hope.

[Resuming questioning the Sausage Seller]

Tell me this—where did you sell sausages,
in the market or at the city gates?

SAUSAGE SELLER

By the gates, where salted foods are sold.

PAPHLAGONIAN *[in tragic style]*

Alas, The god's oracle has been fulfilled!
Roll this ill-fated wretch inside the house.

[He takes of the garland symbolizing his office]

Farewell, my garland, you must now leave me.
With great reluctance I abandon you.
Some other man will now take you up
and will possess you—no greater thief,
but perhaps a man with more good fortune.[139]

[The Paphlagonian tosses the garland away and collapses, lying inert on the ground. The Sausage Seller catches the garland and puts it on his own head.]

SAUSAGE SELLER

O Zeus, god of the Greeks, this victory
belongs to you.

CHORUS LEADER

Hail, glorious conqueror!
Remember that you have become a man
thanks to me. I ask for something trifling—
to be your Phanos and sign your law suits.[140]

DEMOS *[to Sausage Seller]*

Tell me your name.

SAUSAGE SELLER

Agoracritus—
because I was raised on disagreements
in the market.

Δημος

Ἀγορακρίτῳ τοίνυν ἐμαυτὸν ἐπιτρέπω,
καὶ τὸν Παφλαγόνα παραδίδωμι τουτονί.

Αλλαντοπωλης

καὶ μὴν ἐγώ σ' ὦ Δῆμε θεραπεύσω καλῶς,
ὥσθ' ὁμολογεῖν σε μηδέν' ἀνθρώπων ἐμοῦ
ἰδεῖν ἀμείνω τῇ Κεχηναίων πόλει.

Χορος

τί κάλλιον ἀρχομένοισιν
ἢ καταπαυομένοισιν
ἢ θοᾶν ἵππων ἐλατῆρας ἀείδειν, †μηδὲν ἐς† Λυσίστρατον,
μηδὲ Θούμαντιν τὸν ἀνέστιον αὖ λυπεῖν ἑκούσῃ καρδίᾳ;
καὶ γὰρ οὗτος ὦ φίλ' Ἄπολλον ἀεὶ πεινῇ, θαλεροῖς δακρύοις
σᾶς ἁπτόμενος φαρέτρας Πυθῶνι δίᾳ μὴ κακῶς πένεσθαι.

— λοιδορῆσαι τοὺς πονηροὺς οὐδέν ἐστ' ἐπίφθονον,
ἀλλὰ τιμὴ τοῖσι χρηστοῖς, ὅστις εὖ λογίζεται.
εἰ μὲν οὖν ἄνθρωπος, ὃν δεῖ πόλλ' ἀκοῦσαι καὶ κακά,
αὐτὸς ἦν ἔνδηλος, οὐκ ἂν ἀνδρὸς ἐμνήσθην φίλου.
νῦν δ' Ἀρίγνωτον γὰρ οὐδεὶς ὅστις οὐκ ἐπίσταται,
ὅστις ἢ τὸ λευκὸν οἶδεν ἢ τὸν ὄρθιον νόμον.
ἔστιν οὖν ἀδελφὸς αὐτῷ τοὺς τρόπους οὐ συγγενής,
Ἀριφράδης πονηρός. ἀλλὰ τοῦτο μὲν καὶ βούλεται·
ἔστι δ' οὐ μόνον πονηρός, οὐ γὰρ οὐδ' ἂν ᾐσθόμην,
οὐδὲ παμπόνηρος, ἀλλὰ καὶ προσεξηύρηκέ τι.
τὴν γὰρ αὑτοῦ γλῶτταν αἰσχραῖς ἡδοναῖς λυμαίνεται,
ἐν κασωρείοισι λείχων τὴν ἀπόπτυστον δρόσον,
καὶ μολύνων τὴν ὑπήνην καὶ κυκῶν τὰς ἐσχάρας,

DEMOS

Well then, I place myself
in the care of Agoracritus—to him
I hand over the Paphlagonian here.

SAUSAGE SELLER

Demos, I will look after you in style.
You will agree you could not imagine
any man more friendly to this city
full of those who love to yawn and gape.

[Demos and the Sausage Seller go into the house. Some members of the Chorus haul the Paphlagonian off to one side of the stage by his feet and return without him.]

CHORUS

What is more beautiful than to sing
at the start or finish of our choral song
of those who drive swift horses—with no jokes
aimed at Lysistratus and in our hearts
no deliberate wish to harm Thumantis,
who has no home and craves food all the time—
O dear Apollo, with many tears he clings
to thy quiver there in Delphi, begging
not to live in such wretched poverty.[141]

CHORUS LEADER

There is nothing hateful in aiming one's abuse
at wicked rogues—no, if one reasons well
it's paying a tribute to worthwhile citizens.
So if the man about whom we must now proclaim
many bad things were himself well known to all,
I would not mention someone who is my friend.
Now, there is no one who can tell the colour white
from Orthian melodies who does not know
Agrignotus. Well, that man has a brother,
Ariphrades, who in his habits is not like him
and wants to be that way.[142] He is not only bad—
if that were all, I wouldn't pay him any mind—
not only completely nasty, but has invented
something even worse. He corrupts his own tongue
with revolting pleasures, licking disgusting juices
inside the cunts of prostitutes, staining his beard,
stirring up coals in those hot fires, carrying on

καὶ Πολυμνήστεια ποιῶν καὶ ξυνὼν Οἰωνίχῳ.
ὅστις οὖν τοιοῦτον ἄνδρα μὴ σφόδρα βδελύττεται,
οὔ ποτ' ἐκ ταὐτοῦ μεθ' ἡμῶν πίεται ποτηρίου.

— *ἦ πολλάκις ἐννυχίαισι*
φροντίσι συγγεγένημαι,
καὶ διεζήτηχ' ὁπόθεν ποτὲ φαύλως ἐσθίει Κλεώνυμος.
φασὶ μὲν γὰρ αὐτὸν ἐρεπτόμενον τὰ τῶν ἐχόντων ἀνέρων
οὐκ ἂν ἐξελθεῖν ἀπὸ τῆς σιπύης· τοὺς δ' ἀντιβολεῖν ἂν ὅμως·
'ἴθ' ὦ ἄνα πρὸς γονάτων, ἔξελθε καὶ σύγγνωθι τῇ τραπέζῃ.'

— *φασὶν ἀλλήλαις ξυνελθεῖν τὰς τριήρεις ἐς λόγον,*
καὶ μίαν λέξαι τιν' αὐτῶν ἥτις ἦν γεραιτέρα·
'οὐδὲ πυνθάνεσθε ταῦτ' ὦ παρθένοι τἀν τῇ πόλει;
φασὶν αἰτεῖσθαί τιν' ἡμῶν ἑκατὸν ἐς Καρχηδόνα
ἄνδρα μοχθηρὸν πολίτην ὀξίνην Ὑπέρβολον·'
ταῖς δὲ δόξαι δεινὸν εἶναι τοῦτο κοὐκ ἀνασχετόν,
καί τιν' εἰπεῖν ἥτις ἀνδρῶν ἆσσον οὐκ ἐληλύθει·
'ἀποτρόπαι' οὐ δῆτ' ἐμοῦ γ' ἄρξει ποτ', ἀλλ' ἐάν με χρῇ,
ὑπὸ τερηδόνων σαπεῖσ' ἐνταῦθα καταγηράσομαι·'
'οὐδὲ Ναυφάντης γε τῆς Ναύσωνος, οὐ δῆτ' ὦ θεοί,
εἴπερ ἐκ πεύκης γε κἀγὼ καὶ ξύλων ἐπηγνύμην.
ἢν δ' ἀρέσκῃ ταῦτ' Ἀθηναίοις, καθῆσθαί μοι δοκεῖ
ἐς τὸ Θησεῖον πλεούσαις ἢ 'πὶ τῶν σεμνῶν θεῶν.
οὐ γὰρ ἡμῶν γε στρατηγῶν ἐγχανεῖται τῇ πόλει·
ἀλλὰ πλείτω χωρὶς αὐτὸς ἐς κόρακας, εἰ βούλεται,
τὰς σκάφας, ἐν αἷς ἐπώλει τοὺς λύχνους, καθελκύσας.'

ΑΛΛΑΝΤΟΠΩΛΗΣ

εὐφημεῖν χρὴ καὶ στόμα κλῄειν καὶ μαρτυριῶν ἀπέχεσθαι,
καὶ τὰ δικαστήρια συγκλῄειν οἷς ἡ πόλις ἥδε γέγηθεν,

like Polymnestus, and hanging out with Oeonichus.
Any person who does not despise a man like that
will never drink from the same cup as I do.[143]

Chorus

At night certain thoughts often come to me,
and I wonder where Cleonymus gets food
for that voracious appetite he has. They say
that when he grazed on rich men's tables
he'd never leave the tub of food alone.
And they'd keep begging him in unison,
"O lord, by your knees, leave—spare our table."[144]

Chorus Leader

They say our warships once all met together
to chat to one another, and one of them,
an older lady, said, "Girls, don't you realize
what's going on in the city? People are claiming
some man is requisitioning one hundred of us
to sail off to Carthage—some worthless citizen
called sour Hyperbolus."[145] All of them thought this
totally outrageous and would not endure it.
One of those ships, a virgin who'd not yet come near
a crew of men, declared, "May god protect us,
that man will never become my master! Instead,
I'll grow old here, if I must, with festering wood
chewed up by worms." "By the gods, he'll not command
Nauphanta, daughter of Nauson, not if I, too,
am constructed out of pine and timbers. And so,
if Athenians take up Hyperbolus' scheme,
then I think we should hoist sail and seek refuge
at the Theseum or the Furies' sanctuary.
He won't take charge of us and mock the city.
If that's what he wants, let him sail off by himself
and descend to Hades, once he's launched those tubs
he used when trying to sell those lamps of his."[146]

[Enter the Sausage Seller from the house. He is wearing a rich new outfit.]

Sausage Seller

We must maintain a holy silence,
keeping our mouths firmly closed, refraining
from giving evidence, and closing those courts
from which the city gets so much delight.

ἐπὶ καιναῖσιν δ' εὐτυχίαισιν παιωνίζειν τὸ θέατρον.

ΧΟΡΟΣ

ὦ ταῖς ἱεραῖς φέγγος Ἀθήναις καὶ ταῖς νήσοις ἐπίκουρε,
τίν' ἔχων φήμην ἀγαθὴν ἥκεις, ἐφ' ὅτῳ κνισῶμεν
ἀγυιάς;

ΑΛΛΑΝΤΟΠΩΛΗΣ

τὸν Δῆμον ἀφεψήσας ὑμῖν καλὸν ἐξ αἰσχροῦ πεποίηκα.

ΧΟΡΟΣ

καὶ ποῦ 'στιν νῦν ὦ θαυμαστὰς ἐξευρίσκων ἐπινοίας;

ΑΛΛΑΝΤΟΠΩΛΗΣ

ἐν ταῖσιν ἰοστεφάνοις οἰκεῖ ταῖς ἀρχαίαισιν Ἀθήναις.

ΧΟΡΟΣ

πῶς ἂν ἴδοιμεν; ποίαν τιν' ἔχει σκευήν; ποῖος γεγένηται;

ΑΛΛΑΝΤΟΠΩΛΗΣ

οἷός περ Ἀριστείδῃ πρότερον καὶ Μιλτιάδῃ ξυνεσίτει.
ὄψεσθε δέ· καὶ γὰρ ἀνοιγνυμένων ψόφος ἤδη τῶν
προπυλαίων.
ἀλλ' ὀλολύξατε φαινομέναισιν ταῖς ἀρχαίαισιν Ἀθήναις
καὶ θαυμασταῖς καὶ πολυύμνοις, ἵν' ὁ κλεινὸς Δῆμος ἐνοικεῖ.

ΧΟΡΟΣ

ὦ ταὶ λιπαραὶ καὶ ἰοστέφανοι καὶ ἀριζήλωτοι Ἀθῆναι,
δείξατε τὸν τῆς Ἑλλάδος ὑμῖν καὶ τῆς γῆς τῆσδε
μόναρχον.

To salute our new good fortune, people here
should sing a sacred song of gratitude.

Chorus Leader
O you flaming light for sacred Athens
protector of the islands, what good news
do you carry as you move here, for which
we will make our streets fill up with the smell
of smoking sacrifice?

Sausage Seller
I have boiled Demos,
made him young again for you and transformed
something ugly into something beautiful.[147]

Chorus Leader
And so, you fountain of marvellous schemes,
where is he now?

Sausage Seller
He lives in ancient Athens,
that city crowned with violets.

Chorus Leader
How can we see him?
What style of clothing is he wearing?
What sort of man has he become?

Sausage Seller
He has become what he was earlier,
when he lived alongside Aristides
and Miltiades. But you yourselves can see—
for I already hear doors opening
in the Propylaea.[148] Shout out with joy,
as ancient Athens now comes into view,
that wonderful place, so often praised in hymns,
the place where celebrated Demos dwells.

Chorus Leader
Splendid, envied Athens, crowned with violets,
show us the king of all the land of Greece.

[Demos emerges through the doors of the Propylaea. He has been completely rejuvenated and is dressed in traditional clothes.]

ΑΛΛΑΝΤΟΠΩΛΗΣ

ὅδ᾽ ἐκεῖνος ὁρᾶν τεττιγοφόρας, ἀρχαίῳ σχήματι λαμπρός,
οὐ χοιρινῶν ὄζων ἀλλὰ σπονδῶν, σμύρνῃ κατάλειπτος.

ΧΟΡΟΣ

χαῖρ᾽ ὦ βασιλεῦ τῶν Ἑλλήνων· καί σοι ξυγχαίρομεν ἡμεῖς.
τῆς γὰρ πόλεως ἄξια πράττεις καὶ τοῦ ᾽ν Μαραθῶνι
τροπαίου.

ΔΗΜΟΣ

ὦ φίλτατ᾽ ἀνδρῶν ἐλθὲ δεῦρ᾽ Ἀγοράκριτε.
ὅσα με δέδρακας ἀγάθ᾽ ἀφεψήσας.

ΑΛΛΑΝΤΟΠΩΛΗΣ

ἐγώ;
ἀλλ᾽ ὦ μέλ᾽ οὐκ οἶσθ᾽ οἷος ἦσθ᾽ αὐτὸς πάρος,
οὐδ᾽ οἷ᾽ ἔδρας· ἐμὲ γὰρ νομίζοις ἂν θεόν.

ΔΗΜΟΣ

τί δ᾽ ἔδρων, κάτειπέ μοι, πρὸ τοῦ; ποῖός τις ἦ;

ΑΛΛΑΝΤΟΠΩΛΗΣ

πρῶτον μέν, ὁπότ᾽ εἴποι τις ἐν τἠκκλησίᾳ,
᾽ὦ Δῆμ᾽ ἐραστής εἰμι σὸς φιλῶ τέ σε
καὶ κήδομαί σου καὶ προβουλεύω μόνος,᾽
τούτοις ὁπότε χρήσαιτό τις προοιμίοις,
ἀνωρτάλιζες κἀκερουτίας.

ΔΗΜΟΣ

ἐγώ;

ΑΛΛΑΝΤΟΠΩΛΗΣ

εἶτ᾽ ἐξαπατήσας σ᾽ ἀντὶ τούτων ᾤχετο.

ΔΗΜΟΣ

τί φῄς;
ταυτί μ᾽ ἔδρων, ἐγὼ δὲ τοῦτ᾽ οὐκ ᾐσθόμην;

SAUSAGE SELLER

Gaze upon this man, with the cicada
in his hair, glorious in his ancient robes,
anointed with myrrh and smelling now,
not of mussel shells, but offerings of peace.[149]

CHORUS LEADER

Hail king of the Greeks. We rejoice with you.
What you do is worthy of the city
and of our trophy raised at Marathon.[150]

DEMOS

Come here, Agoracritus, dearest of men.
What great things you have done, by boiling me!

SAUSAGE SELLER

I did? My friend, if you do not understand
the kind of person you were previously
and what sort of things you did, you would think
I was a god.

DEMOS

Tell me—what did I do before?
What was I like?

SAUSAGE SELLER

Well, for a start, when someone
announced in the assembly, "O Demos,
I am such an ardent lover of yours,
I am concerned for you and I alone
look out for what you need," at that point—
after someone used these opening phrases—
you'd always flap your wings and toss your horns.

DEMOS

I did that?

SAUSAGE SELLER

Once he'd completely fooled you
merely with these words, he'd go away.

DEMOS

What are you saying? They did that to me,
and I never noticed?

Αλλαντοπωλης

τὰ δ' ὦτά γ' ἄν σου νὴ Δί' ἐξεπετάννυτο
ὥσπερ σκιάδειον καὶ πάλιν ξυνήγετο.

Δημος

οὕτως ἀνόητος ἐγεγενήμην καὶ γέρων;

Αλλαντοπωλης

καὶ νὴ Δί' εἴ γε δύο λεγοίτην ῥήτορε,
ὁ μὲν ποιεῖσθαι ναῦς μακρὰς ὁ δ' ἕτερος αὖ
καταμισθοφορῆσαι τοῦθ', ὁ τὸν μισθὸν λέγων
τὸν τὰς τριήρεις παραδραμὼν ἂν ᾤχετο.
οὗτος τί κύπτεις; οὐχὶ κατὰ χώραν μενεῖς;

Δημος

αἰσχύνομαί τοι ταῖς πρότερον ἁμαρτίαις.

Αλλαντοπωλης

ἀλλ' οὐ σὺ τούτων αἴτιος, μὴ φροντίσῃς,
ἀλλ' οἵ σε ταῦτ' ἐξηπάτων. νυνδὶ φράσον·
ἐάν τις εἴπῃ βωμολόχος ξυνήγορος·
'οὐκ ἔστιν ὑμῖν τοῖς δικασταῖς ἄλφιτα,
εἰ μὴ καταγνώσεσθε ταύτην τὴν δίκην·'
τοῦτον τί δράσεις, εἰπέ, τὸν ξυνήγορον;

Δημος

ἄρας μετέωρον ἐς τὸ βάραθρον ἐμβαλῶ,
ἐκ τοῦ λάρυγγος ἐκκρεμάσας Ὑπέρβολον.

Αλλαντοπωλης

τουτὶ μὲν ὀρθῶς καὶ φρονίμως ἤδη λέγεις·
τὰ δ' ἄλλα, φέρ' ἴδω, πῶς πολιτεύσει φράσον.

SAUSAGE SELLER

Yes. And then, by god,
your ears would open like a parasol
and then close again.

DEMOS

Was I so stupid
and such a dotard?

SAUSAGE SELLER

Yes, by Zeus, you were.
If two orators spoke up, one proposing
to build long ships for war and the other
to spend the same amount to pay off
certain citizens, the one who spoke of pay
would always go away victorious
over the man who spoke of warships.

[Demos turns his head aside.]

Why hang your head? Can't you stand firm here?

DEMOS

Well, I'm ashamed of earlier mistakes.

SAUSAGE SELLER

You shouldn't think about them. Those mistakes
were not your fault—no, they were brought about
by the men who lied to you. Now, tell me,
if some impudent advocate cried out,
"You jury men, there'll be no wheat for you,
unless you convict someone in this case,"
how would you treat the man who made that plea?

DEMOS

I'd string him up above the ground, fling him
into the Barathron, with Hyperbolus
hanging round his neck.[151]

SAUSAGE SELLER

Now you're talking
in a reasonable and proper way.
All right, let's see, what other policies
would you undertake? Tell me.

ΔΗΜΟΣ

πρῶτον μὲν ὁπόσοι ναῦς ἐλαύνουσιν μακράς,
καταγομένοις τὸν μισθὸν ἀποδώσω 'ντελῆ.

ΑΛΛΑΝΤΟΠΩΛΗΣ

πολλοῖς γ' ὑπολίσφοις πυγιδίοισιν ἐχαρίσω.

ΔΗΜΟΣ

ἔπειθ' ὁπλίτης ἐντεθεὶς ἐν καταλόγῳ
οὐδεὶς κατὰ σπουδὰς μετεγγραφήσεται,
ἀλλ' ὥσπερ ἦν τὸ πρῶτον ἐγγεγράψεται.

ΑΛΛΑΝΤΟΠΩΛΗΣ

τοῦτ' ἔδακε τὸν πόρπακα τὸν Κλεωνύμου.

ΔΗΜΟΣ

οὐδ' ἀγοράσει γ' ἀγένειος οὐδεὶς ἐν ἀγορᾷ.

ΑΛΛΑΝΤΟΠΩΛΗΣ

ποῦ δῆτα Κλεισθένης ἀγοράσει καὶ Στράτων;

ΔΗΜΟΣ

τὰ μειράκια ταυτὶ λέγω τἀν τῷ μύρῳ,
ἃ στωμυλεῖται τοιαδὶ καθήμενα·
'σοφός γ' ὁ Φαίαξ δεξιῶς τ' οὐκ ἀπέθανεν.
συνερτικὸς γάρ ἐστι καὶ περαντικός,
καὶ γνωμοτυπικὸς καὶ σαφὴς καὶ κρουστικός,
καταληπτικός τ' ἄριστα τοῦ θορυβητικοῦ.'

ΑΛΛΑΝΤΟΠΩΛΗΣ

οὔκουν καταδακτυλικὸς σὺ τοῦ λαλητικοῦ;

ΔΗΜΟΣ

μὰ Δί' ἀλλ' ἀναγκάσω κυνηγετεῖν ἐγὼ
τούτους ἅπαντας, παυσαμένους ψηφισμάτων.

Demos

First of all,
whenever the long ships return to port,
I will award the rowers their full pay.

Sausage Seller

You'll please many a worn and blistered bum.

Demos

And then, no soldier whose name is entered
on the roll will be transferred somewhere else
because of special interests. It will stay
where it was written down originally.

Sausage Seller

That will sting Cleonymus on his shield band.[152]

Demos

And no one will hang around the marketplace
unless he has a beard.

Sausage Seller

If that's the case,
where will Cleisthenes and Strato buy things?[153]

Demos

By that I mean those young men at the market
where perfumes are sold, who sit there and chat,
saying things like, "That Phaeax is so smart!
The way he escaped death was so clever!
How stylish the man is, how logical,
how good at formulating new expressions,
clear and pointed, and he's the very best
at silencing those nasty hecklers."[154]

Sausage Seller

Surely you'll give these chatterers the finger?

Demos

No, by Zeus. I'll force them all to go hunting
and stop proposing to vote in decrees.

ΑΛΛΑΝΤΟΠΩΛΗΣ

ἔχε νυν ἐπὶ τούτοις τουτονὶ τὸν ὀκλαδίαν,
καὶ παῖδ' ἐνόρχην, ὅσπερ οἴσει τόνδε σοι·
κἄν που δοκῇ σοι, τοῦτον ὀκλαδίαν ποίει.

ΔΗΜΟΣ

μακάριος ἐς τἀρχαῖα δὴ καθίσταμαι.

ΑΛΛΑΝΤΟΠΩΛΗΣ

φήσεις γ', ἐπειδὰν τὰς τριακοντούτιδας
σπονδὰς παραδῶ σοι. δεῦρ' ἴθ' αἱ Σπονδαὶ ταχύ.

ΔΗΜΟΣ

ὦ Ζεῦ πολυτίμηθ' ὡς καλαί· πρὸς τῶν θεῶν,
ἔξεστιν αὐτῶν κατατριακοντουτίσαι;
πῶς ἔλαβες αὐτὰς ἐτέον;

ΑΛΛΑΝΤΟΠΩΛΗΣ

οὐ γὰρ ὁ Παφλαγὼν
ἀπέκρυπτε ταύτας ἔνδον, ἵνα σὺ μὴ λάβῃς;
νῦν οὖν ἐγώ σοι παραδίδωμ' ἐς τοὺς ἀγροὺς
αὐτὰς ἰέναι λαβόντα.

ΔΗΜΟΣ

τὸν δὲ Παφλαγόνα,
ὃς ταῦτ' ἔδρασεν, εἴφ' ὅ τι ποιήσεις κακόν.

ΑΛΛΑΝΤΟΠΩΛΗΣ

οὐδὲν μέγ' ἀλλ' ἢ τὴν ἐμὴν ἕξει τέχνην·
ἐπὶ ταῖς πύλαις ἀλλαντοπωλήσει μόνος,
τὰ κύνεια μιγνὺς τοῖς ὀνείοις πράγμασιν,
μεθύων τε ταῖς πόρναισι λοιδορήσεται,
κἀκ τῶν βαλανείων πίεται τὸ λούτριον.

SAUSAGE SELLER *[beckoning to a slave]*
All right then, given that, accept this stool,
and this slave who will carry it for you.
He's got enormous balls, and if you like,
you can make him your camp stool.

DEMOS
My goodness!
I am reassuming my old habits!

SAUSAGE SELLER
You will claim that for sure when I give you
the peace terms for a truce of thirty years.[155]

[He calls into the house.]

Terms of peace, come out here quickly.

[Enter two scantily clad or perhaps naked young girls whom the Sausage Seller presents to Demos.]

DEMOS
Holy Zeus, they are lovely. By the gods,
can I play around with them for thirty years?
Let me ask you—where did you find them?

SAUSAGE SELLER
Didn't you know the Paphlagonian
was keeping them locked up in the house
where you wouldn't find them? I'm giving them
to you so you can take them with you
when you go back to your country home.

DEMOS
And what about the Paphlagonian
who did all this. How will you punish him?

SAUSAGE SELLER
Nothing excessive. He will carry on
with my old trade beside the city gates,
selling sausages all by himself. He'll keep
making a hash of things, but from now on
with dog and donkey meat. And when he's drunk,
he'll swap his swear words with the prostitutes,
and drink foul water from the public baths.

ΔΗΜΟΣ

εὖ γ' ἐπενόησας οὗπέρ ἐστιν ἄξιος,
πόρναισι καὶ βαλανεῦσι διακεκραγέναι,
καί σ' ἀντὶ τούτων ἐς τὸ πρυτανεῖον καλῶ
ἐς τὴν ἕδραν θ', ἵν' ἐκεῖνος ἦν ὁ φαρμακός.
ἕπου δὲ ταυτηνὶ λαβὼν τὴν βατραχίδα·
κἀκεῖνον ἐκφερέτω τις ὡς ἐπὶ τὴν τέχνην,
ἵν' ἴδωσιν αὐτὸν οἷς ἐλωβᾶθ' οἱ ξένοι.

DEMOS

What you've proposed that man richly deserves,
a slanging match with whores and bath attendants.
And now, in return, I am inviting you
to the Prytaneum, to take the seat
which that piece of filth once occupied.
Put on this frog-green robe and follow me.
Someone take that fellow away from here
where he may ply his trade, so that strangers
whom he used to hurt so much may see him.

[Some of the Chorus haul away the Paphlagonian. Demos, the Sausage Seller, the Peace Treaty Girls, and the Chorus move off towards the city]

NOTES

1 Olympus was a musician from the 7th century who composed flute music. The English words here have been provided by the translator; the Greek simply has them repeating a series of *mu* sounds, without any lyrics.

2 Nicias is here quoting Euripides, a line from *Hippolytus* where Phaedra wishes to confess her passion for her stepson without actually saying the words.

3 Aristophanes is satirizing Euripides' origins by reminding people of the false rumour that his mother, Cleito, sold vegetables. The previous lines also satirize Euripides' style.

4 The punishment for slaves who ran away during wartime was a ferocious whipping. Nonetheless, desertions were not uncommon.

5 The fact that he is so wretched demonstrates that there must be gods. Otherwise he would be better off.

6 The detail about chewing beans may be a reference to Demos' crude habits. Some commentators see an allusion here to the use of beans to count votes in the election of public officials.

7 Paphlagonia is a remote, rugged area on the southern shores of the Black Sea. The reference to a "tanner" identifies the slave for the audience as Cleon, a powerful politician and general in Athens, whose family derived their wealth from a tanning business. He was not from Paphlagonia. That word, however, also alludes to a blustery style of speech. Cleon was an opponent of the richer, aristocratic classes and was very aggressive in prosecuting the war with Sparta.

8 This is an invitation to Demos to cut short his public duties at the law court and enjoy the pleasures of a bath and food, while still taking the full fee for his services. Three obols was the daily amount given for jury duty (Cleon had had the amount increased from two obols). The phrase "tiny bits of leather" is alleging that Cleon distributes small bribes to get his way with Demos (the people).

9 In 425 BC (the year before the production of *Knights*) the Athenian general Demosthenes had engineered a military triumph against the Spartans at Pylos. Cleon had come out in the final stages of the campaign and together he and Demosthenes had inflicted a major defeat on the Spartans. Cleon received almost all the credit for the victory and, as a result, was extremely popular.

10 Hylas is a common name for a slave.

11 The Chaones are a group living in north-west Greece. The Greek names for these places bring out certain double meanings which are lost in translation (except perhaps for the pun Cahones-cojones). Aetolia sounds like the Greek word meaning to demand, and Clopidae, a small part of Athens, sounds as if it comes from the Greek word for thief. The basic satiric point is that Cleon's reach is extensive and corrupt everywhere.

12 Themistocles was a leading Athenian politician at the time of the Persian invasions and played a decisive role in the Persian defeat in 480 BC. Bull's blood was believed to be poisonous. However, there is no reliable evidence that Themistocles died from drinking it.

13 After dinner a libation of unmixed wine was made to the Good Spirit (i.e., Dionysus). In the regular drinking which followed the libation, the wine was mixed with water.

14 A libation is an offering to a god in which a small amount of liquid (usually wine) is poured out onto the ground or an altar. Nicias suspects Demosthenes is simply going to drink the wine; hence, the latter reassures him that he wants the wine for a religious purpose. Ancient Greeks normally drank wine mixed with water.

15 The term *Pramnian* refers to a wine of good quality produced in different places.

16 The oracles are prophecies written out on scrolls.

17 Bacis was a well-known contemporary prophet, who is said to have predicted many events of the war. There is also a pun on Bacchus, the god of wine.

18 The dealer in hemp is Eucrates, an Athenian politician, who opposed and was removed from power by Cleon.

19 The sheep dealer is a reference to Lysicles, who was killed in a military action in 428 BC. The repeated notion of political leaders who first make money from common trades, as Sommerstein suggests, is emphasizing a new breed of politician in the state, a middle-class merchant who uses his money to gain political influence and power.

20 The Cycloborus was a stream near Athens which turned into a noisy torrent in the spring.

21 The Greek says "up here," because Demosthenes is on a stage, above the orchestra where the Sausage Seller enters.

22 Merry notes that the salute would be with the thumb and forefinger touching the lips, a gesture made at a moment of great good fortune.

23 The Pnyx is a large amphitheatre west of the Acropolis in Athens where the Athenian assembly met. The Prytaneum was the symbolic centre of civic life, a building where a sacred fire was kept and important figures were entertained. Citizens who had given exceptional service to the state could gain the privilege of eating there at public expense. Sommerstein notes that the sexual depravity is a swipe at Athenian politicians and an indication of the Sausage Seller's fitness for public office, since he does not object to the gross insult which calls him, in effect, a public prostitute.

24 Caria is a city on the east coast of Asia Minor, and Carthage is far to the west of Athens. The Sausage Seller is being asked to survey virtually the whole eastern and central Mediterranean. Neither Caria nor Carthage is part of the Athenian empire, but some ambitious politicians were hoping to extend that empire in both directions.

25 This seems to mean, as Sommerstein points out, that the serpent-sausage maker will prevail, unless he is intimidated by Cleon's bluster. Green notes (following Walsh) that the mention of blood suggests that the sausages may be more like black pudding than conventional sausages.

26 This is either a joke at Cleon's expense (his face is so hideous and terrifying that artists are too scared to create a likeness) or else, as Sommerstein suggests, Aristophanes may have had legal reasons for not depicting Cleon visually (or using his name in the play). Given the comic possibilities of a mask, it seems odd that one is not used for the Paphlagonian. According to tradition, Aristophanes may have played the part of the Paphlagonian himself with his face smeared with ochre and wine-lees.

27 The cup Demosthenes has been using is made of silver from Chalcis. The Paphlagonian immediately concludes they must be fomenting a revolt against Athens in the region of Chalcis.

28 Charybdis was a destructive whirlpool which sucked everything down into it. In *Odyssey* 12 it is an important hazard Odysseus and his crew must cope with.

29 The precise meaning of this line is obscure. Merry notes that it might refer to the fact that Eucrates, once he was driven from political power by Cleon, went back to being a commercially successful bran merchant. Green suggests that it might be based on a well-known event when Eucrates escaped danger by hiding under a pile of bran.

30 Outgoing public officials had to have their use of public money checked by an audit, a process which, so this states, Cleon abused.

31 I follow Merry and Sommerstein and others in placing lines 264 and 265 of the Greek text between lines 260 and 261. The Chersonese is a distant region to the north-east of Athens, in Thrace. The suggestion seems to be that the Athenian citizen had gone there for a peaceful, non-political life.

32 There is some doubt over the speaker of these lines. Along with other editors, I assign them to the Sausage Seller, since he must enter the argument at some point, and assigning this speech to the Chorus Leader, as the manuscript does, creates a staging problem.

33 A honey cake was a prize at a drinking party for the best performer and for the one who stayed awake the longest.

34 Pericles was the political leader in Athens at the height of its glory. He died of the plague a year after war broke out. These lines apparently mean that he never received the honour of dining at public expense at the Prytaneum. They also suggest that whoever did have that honour was not entitled to take food away with him.

35 In other words, I'm just as capable of putting a bold face on things as you are.

36 The Greek uses the word *Prytanes*, which, as Sommerstein notes, is the business committee of the City Council. He also suggests that with the phrase "sacred tripe" the Paphlagonian may be stating that the Sausage Seller's wares are spoils of war and thus subject to tax.

37 Merry notes that in coastal regions people on land kept watch for shoals of tuna fish.

38 The leather was cut obliquely so as to look thick and strong, but it was so bad it quickly expanded, and the shoes no longer fit.

39 Pergase was a community close to Athens. Hence, the trip to it would be a short walk.

40 Hippodamus' son is Archeptolemus, a well-known politician. From this reference it would appear that he is opposed to Cleon's aggressive war policies but is doing nothing about them. Merry mentions that Archeptolemus was probably in the audience, so that the phrase "watching in tears" takes on an added significance.

41 The place where the "worthy" men are brought up now is, of course, the marketplace.

42 Merry notes that winning a case in court against a foreigner was probably easier than winning one against an Athenian citizen.

43 Miletus was famous for its sea bass. Sommerstein suggests the speech may have something to do with Cleon's accepting a bribe from the Milesians and then ignoring them.

44 The rich silver mines in Attica were owned by the state but leased to individuals. The implication is that he will use his political influence to make himself very rich.

45 Cooks checked on the health of a pig by forcing its mouth open, pushing its tongue aside, and checking for spots. An unsatisfactory pig, Merry notes, had white spots. Here the sense is that if they followed this procedure with Cleon, they'll be able to see right down to his anus to check it for disease.

46 The grain crop is a reference to the Spartan prisoners captured in the victory in the Peloponnese (for which Cleon saw to it that he received all the credit). He had these men (120 in all) brought back to Athens and thrown into prison under desperate conditions, without sufficient water or food. The suggestion here is that he is negotiating to ransom them for profit.

47 Cratinus, a successful comic poet, is a frequent target of Aristophanic satire. He was, by reputation, a notorious drinker. Hence, the fleece or blanket on which he slept would be frequently soaked in urine. I have

made that reference more explicit than it is in the Greek (by adding the phrase about the thighs). Morsimus was a tragic poet Aristophanes often attacks for his wretched poetry.

48 The reference here is obscure. The best conjecture is that the lines refer to someone called Ulius, a man in charge of checking wheat supplies, who was a lover of young boys. In the Greek there is possibly a pun involved on "watching the grain" and "looking out for boys." Ulius will be happy if Cleon repents, because then less food will be stolen. Sommerstein points out that there is historical evidence for a man called Ulius of about the right age.

49 The offerings to Zeus were part of the rites performed in honour of Zeus at the opening of the Public Assembly. The statement indicates that the Paphlagonian would no longer take part in the Assembly (i.e., give up political life).

50 Diners cleaned their fingers by wiping them on pieces of bread, which were then fed to dogs.

51 Merry notes that nettles in salad were tasty only at the very beginning of spring. The Athenians made much of the arrival of the first swallows, a sign of the arrival of spring.

52 Potidaea was a city which had surrendered to Athens some years before after a long siege. The accusation is that the Paphlagonian accepted a huge bribe to argue for more generous peace terms. A talent was worth many thousands of dollars in today's money.

53 Part of the line is missing. I follow Sommerstein's suggestion for the missing words. The inserted phrase is in square brackets.

54 The Paphlagonian is accusing the Sausage Seller that he comes from an aristocratic family who, many years before, had murdered some political refugees who had taken refuge in the Temple of Athena, after promising them safety. The family was still considered under a curse.

55 Hippias, who ruled Athens at the end of the 6th century (i.e., long before), was a tyrant. He remained a symbol of anti-democratic practices. His wife's name was Myrsine. The change of name to *Bursina*, Green suggests, may be an attempt at a pun on *bursa*, the Greek word for *hide*, a reference to Cleon's business in leather.

56 Argos, an important city state in the central Peloponnese, was officially neutral at the start of the war. Winning that state to one's cause would be a natural and important strategy.

57 Demosthenes is upset because the Sausage Seller has not responded to the Paphlagonian's use of the language of carpentry. The Greek uses the word meaning "wheelwright." I have substituted a more general term ("building trades"). The placement of this line varies, but, as Merry and Sommerstein and others note, this seems to be the most obvious place for it.

58 The allegation here is that Cleon is arranging some private deal for the ransom of the Spartan prisoners mentioned earlier (the ones he had brought back to Athens after the Athenian victory in the Peloponnese).

59 The general Demosthenes had been involved in negotiations with democratic citizens in the city state of Boeotia, trying to win that region over to the Athenian cause. Cleon is accusing him of consorting with the enemy. I have used the phrase "making hay" (meaning "work for one's own advantage") in place of the Greek verb which refers to making cheese.

60 Fighting cocks were given garlic to make them fight more aggressively. Demosthenes continues the metaphor of the cockfight in his next speech.

61 In this passage, which announces a shift in tone to a more serious passage, the Greek says "listen to our anapaests." But since that is not the rhythm in the English, I have substituted "formal verse" and switched to hexameters.

62 Aristophanes' earlier plays were produced by other people and not under his own name. Usually a playwright would request the appropriate official to name a sponsor who would pay for the production.

63 Magnes was an earlier comic poet who had recently died.

64 Merry notes that Magnes had written plays featuring harp players, birds, frogs, Lydians, and gall flies.

65 Cratinus (519 BC to 422 BC) was an important comic playwright and rival of Aristophanes.

66 The "sandals of figs" is a parody of a Homeric phrase "sandals of gold." And the phrase contains in Greek an allusion to *sycophant*(meaning *a servile flatterer*), a word put together from *sykon* (*fig*) and *phanein* (*show*).

67 Connus was a well-known and successful musician who, in his old age, was very poor.

68 The name Dionysus refers to a statue of the god in the theatre.

69 Crates was a successful writer of comic dramas. There is a criticism here that Crates' productions were relatively cheap (as Sommerstein observes) and insufficiently ribald.

70 The Lenaean feast is the festival at which the comic dramas were staged. The reference to the poet's forehead may be a reference to Aristophanes' baldness. The Greek here involves an elliptical metaphor taken from rowing, in which the audience is urged to applaud with "eleven oars." Green suggests this may refer to a galley with eleven oars on each side used in a naval escort honouring someone. I have substituted the phrase "all of your fingers."

71 Sunium and Geraestus were promontories, important landmarks for sailors. Phormio was a very successful Athenian naval commander. The Athenian supremacy at sea was one of their most important military advantages in the war with the Spartans.

72 At the Panathenaea festival a sacred robe was carried in a procession to the temple of Athena in the Acropolis, where it was placed on the statue of the goddess.

73 None of the older generals would have expected to be rewarded with free meals at the Prytaneum. Now, generals try to get that privilege through Cleaenetus, Cleon's father.

74 Long hair was fashionable among rich young men who made up the ranks of the Knights and a sign of social snobbery. Keeping the body well scrubbed is a sign of frequent bathing and, Merry suggests, might be considered effeminate.

75 The victory mentioned refers to the competition to win first place in the drama contest.

76 Here the chorus of Knights imagines that the horses have human qualities so that they can pay tribute, in effect, to themselves.

77 The Chorus here is referring to a cavalry expedition against Corinth, an ally of Sparta, in the previous year. It is not clear who Theorus was. Sommerstein suggests he may be an associate of Cleon's. Green states that the word *crab* was a derogatory label for a Corinthian.

78 This remark is parodying Homer where thunder on the right is a favourable message from the gods.

79 The barrier separated the public from the members of the Council.

80 If there were no bowls available for the public, then people would not purchase sardines, because they would have no way of transporting them, and thus the price would stay low.

81 The Presidents (Prytaneis) were a special committee of 50 members of the Council. The archers were the security forces guarding the Council.

82 The Greek says, "I can make Demos wide or narrow." Sommerstein points out that this must be a proverbial expression meaning "I can do anything I like with Demos."

83 The harvest wreath, Merry explains, is a garland of twigs and olive and wool interwoven with fruits and berries. It was used in certain festivals and then placed on the front door.

84 It is not entirely clear what this metaphor refers to. Whatever the reference, the comparison involves a picture of open-mouthed stupidity.

85 The lead weights (called "dolphins" because of their shape) were raised high and then dropped on the deck of the enemy ship in order to shatter its timbers.

86 Lysicles was a political figure in Athens who had died in the war. He lived with Pericles' mistress after Pericles died of the plague. Cynna and Salabaccha were well-known prostitutes. I have added the word "sluts" to make that more explicit.

87 Kerameikos is a region of Athens. Sommerstein notes that it was the area with the largest cemeteries, so that the Sausage Seller may be saying he'll be hauled off for burial.

88 In the Battle of Marathon (490 BC) an army of Greek states led by Athenians defeated the Persian force, a highlight of Athenian history. In the Battle of Salamis (480 BC) the Persians were defeated at sea, one of a series of defeats which ended the second Persian invasion. The "arse that did so well" in the battle was the backside of each man

on the rowing benches, which, as Merry remarks, had a thin cushion underneath it.

89 Harmodius and his brother in 514 had assassinated a brother of the tyrant Hippias. His name became synonymous with Athenians who loved democracy and would fight for it.

90 The war broke out in 431 BC, seven years earlier, but the various provocations which initiated war started earlier than that. The mention of cramped living conditions refers to the fact that in the early part of the war, the countryside was left undefended and all the country folk came to take refuge in Athens, so that there was an acute shortage of living space. The Spartans sought terms of peace after the defeat at Pylos. Archeptolemus was probably one of the negotiators.

91 Arcadia is a large region in the Peloponnese. Hence, the implication is that the Athenian people will one day take over that territory and that jurymen will be paid more.

92 Small stones were used to tally the votes in the assembly. Sommerstein points out that Cleon wanted the war to continue, because once it ended the country people would return to their land and realize how much they had lost thanks to the warmongers like Cleon.

93 It is not clear what walls Cleon built. Themistocles was responsible for the long walls which joined Athens and the port of Pireus in one defensive unit. Themistocles was condemned to exile from Athens for running away when charged with treason. The barley cake is called in the Greek "Achillean," a reference to its superior quality. The fact that Cleon uses such fine cake as a napkin to wipe his fingers on is a sign of his extravagance in a time of war.

94 Mytilene, a city in the Athenian alliance, rebelled against Athens. The Athenians reacted savagely. Cleon was particularly vehement in proposing vicious punishments against the city. The bribe (a relatively small amount) may have been to get him to mitigate his proposals.

95 The trident is associated with Poseidon, god of the sea and of earthquakes.

96 The shields of the Spartans captured at Pylos were set up as trophies and put on display. Green notes that when shields were hung up in this way, their straps were normally removed.

97 Playing around with broken pottery refers to a children's pastime, but it also evokes the practice of ostracism (from the word *ostraka*, the piece of broken pottery used in the voting), by which an Athenian citizen could be exiled for ten years after a vote in the Assembly.

98 Sommerstein notes that any citizen who was a male prostitute could have his name stricken from the voting rolls. It is not clear who Gryttus refers to.

99 The *business with Piraeus* was the decision to fortify Piraeus and build the long walls, so that Athens and its harbour would form a single defensive unit. Themistocles was the moving spirit behind that idea.

100 Merry explains that at a drinking party the slippers were left in the hall. Someone in a hurry to go to the toilet might take any pair of slippers.

101 Silphium was a common herb in the Athenian diet.

102 The Greek place named in the text is *Kopros* (meaning *dung*), an urban area close to Athens.

103 The Greek text says "worthy of Pyrrhandrus," a reference which is unclear. The first part of the name means *red* or *tawny*. I have substituted the notion of catching someone "red handed."

104 The military leaders appointed commanders of warships, who had to supply and repair the ships, an expensive matter.

105 The Sausage Seller is here comparing the Paphlagonian to a boiling pot which needs some of the hot liquid removed. The word *ladle* is not in the Greek, but the Sausage Seller, as Merry suggests (following Green), could produce one from his equipment.

106 Merry points out that property taxes were first imposed during the war when the treasury was in dire need of money. The amount paid depended on a person's wealth.

107 The sea gull (or cormorant) was synonymous with gluttony.

108 Cleonymus, a favourite target of Aristophanes, was an ally of Cleon's and an Athenian general. He had a reputation as a coward and a glutton.

109 Smicythos is a man known for his effeminate ways. His husband would be with him in the court since a woman could not represent herself in a lawsuit.

110 These two implements are for breaking things down and mixing them up; hence, they are associated with Cleon's style of politics. Note that this is the only time the name Cleon is mentioned in the play.

111 Merry notes that the Dorian style was more serious than the passionate Phrygian style and the more lyrical Lydian style.

112 The final lines involve an untranslatable Greek pun linking Dorian to *dora*, meaning *bribes* or *gifts*, suggesting that Cleon would only play the Dorian style because he loved bribes so much, even as a young boy.

113 This mention of an eagle is a reference to a famous oracle of Bacis which promised eternal greatness to Athens.

114 Phoebus is another name for Apollo. Erechtheus was a legendary king of Athens. His descendants or sons are the Athenians.

115 Cerberus is the dog guarding the entrance to the underworld.

116 In the Greek there is a relatively feeble joke on the name Antileon (meaning *instead of a lion*). Sommerstein states that Antileon is the name of a tyrant from Chalcis. With the name *Simba* and the word *symbol* I have tried to provide some equally feeble English humour.

117 Loxias is a common name for Apollo.

118 The wooden stocks have separate holes for each hand, each foot, and the head.

119 Cecrops was another legendary king of Athens. His sons are the Athenians.

120 There was a well known verse ("There is a Pylos before Pylos, and there is another Pylos besides") which refers to the fact that there were a number of places in the Peloponnese called Pylos, all claiming to be the original city ruled by Nestor in Homer's *Iliad*. The Paphlagonian is obviously keen to keep mentioning his great military success in the war.

121 The Greek joke turns on a similarity between the sound of *Pylos* (the place) and *puelos* (meaning *a bath tub*).

122 Philostratus was a pimp whose nickname was Dog Fox.

123 The fast ships collecting cash are the ones sent around to the allies of Athens to collect the money they owe for their alliance.

124 Merry notes that Athenian soldiers who had not been paid foraged for food on the farms.

125 Leto's son is Apollo. The Greek names the port Cyllene, a place in Elis, which leads to the pun on the word *kullos*, meaning *deformed* or *crooked.*

126 Diopeithes was known for his extreme religious views, but there is no evidence he was corrupt or that he had a deformed hand (a characteristic which would seem to be demanded by the dialogue).

127 Merry notes that by the name Red Sea Aristophanes is referring to the Indian Ocean and that Ecbatana, the capital of Media, is synonymous with enormous wealth and power.

128 Thuphanes was a minor public official and a crony of Cleon's.

129 The *victims of state* or *public victims* were slaves or captives or prisoners who were kept to be sacrificed as scapegoats in a ritual designed to protect the state.

130 The top of the voting urn or ballot box was shaped like a funnel.

131 Merry notes that the stage business here involves a race, with the Paphlagonian and the Sausage Seller having chests of food and various goods in different places (on either side of the stage), and Demos having a central position in between the two. Hence, there is a lot of activity involved in the running to and fro.

132 The statue of Athena in the Parthenon was 33 feet high. Hence, the hands on the goddess were immense. Scooped out bread crusts were used as spoons for soup. Green notes that the line makes better sense if the bread crust is very large so that the part scooped out with a finger is quite big.

133 There is a pun in the Greek involving the word for *cake* and the word for *row.* I have tried to provide some equivalent with the pun on currants/currents.

134 The Greeks rarely drank undiluted wine. A solution of two parts wine to three parts water was common.

135 Athena was commonly called Tritogeneia. It is not clear what the word means but etymologically it could have something to do with the number three (e.g. thrice born, born third). Hence, the link to the wine-and-water mixture.

136 Merry explains that hare was considered a delicacy in Athens but that during the war they were very scarce, since the Spartans occupied much of the countryside and there were restrictions on imports (hence the later mention of a risk involved).

137 The *symbol of office* (in the Greek a *garland*) would be something like an official wreath on his head.

138 This is a quotation from the *Telephus* of Euripides.

139 These lines, in a parody of tragic style, echo a lament in Euripides' tragedy *Alcestis*.

140 The Chorus Leader is asking to work for the Sausage Seller by helping him initiate law suits and prosecutions. Phanos performed this work for Cleon. The speech is sometimes assigned to Demosthenes. There is some justification for that, since he first recruited the Sausage Seller, but his reappearance here is dramatically awkward, because he has been absent for so long and has no other lines.

141 Lysistratus was apparently a well-known pauper in Athens. Thumantis was, one assumes from this passage, an Athenian very down on his luck. The passage seems to mean that at this moment we wish to celebrate ourselves (as Knights) rather than satirize the less fortunate.

142 Agrignotus was a musician popular in Athens. His brother Ariphrades, Sommerstein notes, is a frequent target of Aristophanes.

143 Polymnestus and Oeonichus are, one assumes, known figures in Athens. We have no knowledge of their personal habits apart from this reference.

144 Cleonymus, an Athenian politician, is one of the most frequently attacked targets in Aristophanes' plays, usually for his gluttony or his cowardice.

145 Hyperbolus, another favourite target of Aristophanes, was an up-and-coming politician in Athens. His commercial business was selling lamps. The most ambitious of the war-mongering Athenians, as mentioned before, had lofty imperial ambitions to extend the Athenian empire to Carthage, in North Africa.

146 The Theseum, the Temple of Theseus, Merry notes, was a famous sanctuary, where slaves took refuge from cruel masters. The Temple of the Furies was a shrine in Athens. Since these were in the city, Sommerstein observes, the ships could not literally sail there.

147 Merry notes that this mention of boiling is a reference to the famous story in which Medea, a queen with magical powers, rejuvenates Pelias, an old man, in her cauldron.

148 Aristides and Miltiades were celebrated Athenian leaders in the days of the Persian Wars. The Propylaea is the entrance to the Acropolis in Athens. Presumably we are to assume that Demos' house has now become that symbol of democratic government. The Acropolis of Aristophanes' time did not exist during the Persian Wars. Sommerstein suggests that at this point a platform is rolled out of the doors of the house with a structure on it symbolizing the Propylaea of ancient Athens.

149 The cicada brooch worn in the hair was a mark of traditional styles of dress, long out of fashion. Mussel shells were used in the law courts as voting tokens.

150 Marathon was the site of the famous victory against the first Persian expedition in 490 BC.

151 The Barathron was a natural gully into which criminals were thrown.

152 Citizens eligible for military service had their names written on a list and were conscripted in order, but it was possible to use one's influence to get the position of the name changed and thus to evade having to fight. Cleonymus, a common target of Aristophanes, had a reputation as a coward.

153 Cleisthenes is often satirized as a beardless and effeminate man. Strato is linked to him elsewhere in Aristophanes as another immature man without a beard.

154 Phaeax was a well known orator in Athens.

155 Athens had secured a thirty-year truce with the Spartans in 445 BC.

www.ingramcontent.com/pod-product-compliance
Lightning Source LLC
Chambersburg PA
CBHW060924040426
42445CB00011B/784

* 9 7 8 1 9 4 0 9 9 7 9 5 7 *